WOMEN, WORK, AND POLITICS

THE INSTITUTION FOR SOCIAL AND POLICY STUDIES
AT YALE UNIVERSITY

THE YALE ISPS SERIES

WOMEN, WORK, AND POLITICS

The Political Economy
of Gender Inequality

Torben Iversen and
Frances Rosenbluth

Yale UNIVERSITY PRESS
New Haven & London

Yale University Press books may be purchased in quantity for
educational, business, or promotional use. For information, please e-mail
sales.press@yale.edu (U.S. office) or sales@yaleup.co.uk (U.K. office).

Set in Galliard type by The Composing Room of Michigan, Inc.
Printed in the United States of America.

Library of Congress Cataloging-in-Publication Data

Iversen, Torben.
    Women, work, and politics : the political economy of gender inequality /
Torben Iversen, Frances Rosenbluth.
       p. cm. (The Yale ISPS Series)
    Includes bibliographical references and index.
    ISBN 978-0-300-15310-1 (cloth : alk. paper)
       1. Women—Political activity—United States.   2. Women and
democracy—United States.   3. Women—Economic conditions—
United States.   4. Women—Employment—United States.   5. Sexual
division of labor.   I. Rosenbluth, Frances McCall.   II. Title.
    HQ1236.I96 2010
    305.420973—dc22

                                                            2010001860

A catalogue record for this book is available from the Library of
Congress and the British Library.

This paper meets the requirements of ANSI/NISO Z39.48-1992
(Permanence of Paper).

10 9 8 7 6 5 4 3 2 1

CONTENTS

PREFACE

Why is it that women are still so far behind men in the exercise of power? Even in rich democracies, women are underrepresented in government legislatures and corporate boardrooms, earn less than men for comparable work, and are significantly more likely to live below the poverty line. This inequality extends into the private sphere of the family, where a third or more of society's work, unaccounted for in official statistics, is performed almost entirely by women.

This book provides an answer to that question. Part of our answer can be traced to the simple fact that women often take time off or slow down their careers to have children. For a comparably intelligent and educated man and woman employed in a job at which they can become better over time—because, for example, they come to understand the way the firm and market work, or because they build useful relationships within and outside the firm—the woman's career suffers if she quits her job or slows down while her children are young. But even women who don't take time off for child rearing are affected. *All* women are less likely to be hired or promoted in those kinds of jobs because on average, even in the twenty-first century, women are far more likely to slow down during the child-bearing years. From the standpoint of employers, women represent a bigger risk and a correspondingly worse investment in human capital. Discrimination against women—because as a group women are less productive—does not require prejudice to be efficient, and it is widely practiced.

It is hard to think of a serious career in which a worker's productivity cannot be hurt significantly by taking off or cutting back for a few years. In finance, insurance, and law, suspended careers or curtailed hours can mean the loss of client portfolios to colleagues with greater availability. Business managers fail at their jobs unless they can regularly monitor markets and personnel and respond nimbly to new developments. In high-tech careers, it is hard to recover after falling behind technological developments. In academe, a bigger load of family work can translate into lower productivity, impaired academic standing, and lower salaries. In government legislatures that distribute powerful committee positions according to seniority, women who take time for motherhood find themselves farther back in line than men their own age. Regardless of her talents and energy, a woman who leaves her career midstream with the intention of returning later loses momentum. The hit to a woman's employment value from career interruption is lower, of course, at the bottom of the skills continuum: routine clerical work, food service jobs, bookkeeping, lower school teaching, child care, housecleaning, and some manual labor jobs. If women in fast-track jobs drop out while women in menial jobs are less pressured to do so, the net effect is that women find themselves huddled at the bottom of the economic stack, gender-equal education notwithstanding.

One measure of the cost of motherhood is the negative relationship between income and fertility. Regardless of education, women—though not men—earn less as they have more children. To put it another way, a woman who wants to maximize her income would have to think twice about having children in a way that a man never would. And as we've already noted, women are docked for the productivity losses associated with childbearing and other family work even when they choose not to have a family at all. Although equal employment legislation forbids it, employers find ways to protect themselves from the costs associated with widely accepted female roles in family life, essentially slapping on a "mommy penalty" to anyone without a Y chromosome.

None of this would matter a great deal, perhaps, if we could think of families rather than individuals as the relevant social actors. Members of a family love and care for each other, and as long as men and women pool their income, spending power evens out. From this perspective, a sharp division of labor may even maximize welfare. But in countries like today's

America, where one out of two couples dissolves somewhere on the way between altar and grave—or even in countries where divorce is low but men spend their resources on other women—the image of the family as a welfare-maximizing unit loses contact with reality. Having invested all your time and talents in the family is an obvious disadvantage when the family dissolves. Thus women, on average, have more to lose from a breakup than men.

We do not imagine that the possibility of desertion inserts itself into every decision involving family resources. The effect of asymmetric power to leave a marriage is likely to be far more subtle, internalized as social norms and expectations about who does what around the house. In a household where the man has greater average earning capacity, the woman has a larger stake in keeping the marriage as a going concern. This is empirically measurable by the larger share of family work that she performs around the house, even when she works as many hours outside the home as her husband. One way to interpret this—though possibly not the way she interprets it to herself—is that the work she does is proportional to the amount her living standards would drop if the family were to break up. We find empirically that the greater the woman's wages and education level—which captures something of her market power—the less extra work she does around the house; conversely, the longer she has been out of the labor market, the more grunt work she does at home. Yet in all cases, the woman does more of the work than the man, which is difficult to explain in the absence of social conventions.

This snapshot of gender inequality piques our curiosity rather than satisfies it. It leaves unanswered the question of where the inequality came from in the first place, where it is going, and how it varies across countries or sectors of the economy. The gender division of labor, women's representation in politics, and gender norms vary conspicuously across time and place. Since women's childbearing and -rearing responsibilities are largely constant, these variations present something of a mystery.

No one, from our perspective of political economy, offers a compelling explanation for differences in gender inequality. Socialization is a primary transmission mechanism because families teach their sons and daughters to fit into roles that society has laid out for them, but socialization is an effect of inequality, not its cause. Where do these roles come from in the first place, and why are they more or less universal? If gendered roles in family life place women at a disadvantage in earning market income, how did we end up with that division of labor? In our view, a large part of the explanation rests on differences in male and female productivity in market labor. In systems of economic production in which having a baby and leaving the labor market for a period of time does not impair productivity while in work, the demand for female labor should match that of men, and by extension, so should her bargaining power within the home. But when child birth significantly reduces a woman's market productivity, the low demand for female labor means that she is unable to live without male patronage, weakening her standing in the home. When such inequality persists, socialization follows suit. Parents who want the best for their children teach their daughters—as well as sons—to be strong and self-confident when there is demand for their labor. But when women's labor has lesser value, daughters are taught to behave in ways that are pleasing to fathers and husbands to whose largesse they are beholden.

In this book we will show how gender inequality is shaped by the interactions between women's roles as caregivers and their productivity in different economic systems, from the hunter-gatherer and agricultural societies that have existed throughout most of human history to different types of industrial and postindustrial societies. In many pre-agricultural societies, women collected as much as three-quarters of the community's daily caloric intake in the form of plants and small animals while men specialized in the high-risk, high-return job of hunting large game. To the extent that women were able to carry children with them as they gathered or could rely on kin to help care for them, their childbearing role did not rob them of their source of livelihood. With less need of a male patron to survive, women were in a stronger bargaining position within the family and, by extension, the community. Families in such settings need not teach their daughters that marriage (or the equivalent) is destiny, and gender relations can be relatively equal.

The sharp differentiation in male and female roles likely arrived along with sedentary agriculture. The gradual shift to labor-intensive cultivation and protection of single-family land plots put women at a physical disadvantage relative to men in securing their own livelihood. It is a rule of thumb that small changes in comparative advantage can produce large effects in the allocation of resources, and gender inequality is no exception. Men are on average only about 15 percent larger and stronger than women, and women are incapacitated by childbirth for relatively short periods. But for communities living at the edge of survival, these small differences sufficed to push families to allocate roles in the most productive way possible. The power of social norms is to transform small biological differences into gender roles with enormous consequences for who gets what. The male comparative advantage in brawn was accentuated by growing land scarcity, which increased the value not only of a man's labor but also of his ability to defend the farm against marauders. Women also performed back-breaking farm labor, but their work in the field was supplemental to men's. Cultural and religious precepts that relegated women primarily to household work may have encoded the wisdom of the ages, but economic efficiency came at the cost of gender equality, since in this arrangement only men had mobile resources. If he chose to leave his marriage, a man had his farming skills and knowledge and possibly property as well, whereas a woman making a similar decision would forfeit her investment in children and the household. A future partner would not regard her children as an asset, and in any case, children were property that remained with the father. Yet it is a testimony to the limits of male power that marriage in most cultures became a sacred institution, and that there were strong norms against abandoning wife and children. Men enjoyed greater privileges, but their freedom was not unbounded.

Then came the industrial revolution. The forklift made a 120-pound woman as strong as a 180-pound man, creating the potential to upend gender inequality. Mechanization of work that had formerly required male brawn reduced men's productivity edge over women in the labor market. Yet while factories did hire women (and children), the demand for female labor did not rise to parity with men. For one thing, much unskilled work still required muscle power to move mortar, steel, and big machinery around. For those who received significant training, skills tended to be specific to firms and industries, and this made uninterrupted careers a priority for employers who invested in skilled workers. Male workers, who could more credibly commit to continuous careers, had an advantage in competing for skilled jobs. Many kinds of industrial work, particularly in coordinated market economies of Europe, relied on heavy investment in specific skills, and this put women at a distinct disadvantage. Women owe their entry into the industrial labor market almost entirely to the introduction of mass production techniques, which created a number of unskilled routine jobs around the assembly line that women could compete for.

But the industrial revolution's main impact on gender relations came via the unprecedented number of service jobs it created. One of the starkest empirical findings of this book is that gender equality in any given country—as measured by female labor force participation, wage equality, and gender norms—is more strongly correlated with the size of the country's service sector than its industrial sector. Moreover, economics matters more than politics. Postindustrial countries are also the world's oldest democracies, but among rich democracies, gender equality is uncorrelated with the duration of female suffrage. The evolution of economic productivity is what has transformed societal norms and practices. The demand for female labor in the service sector followed from these jobs' lower costs of career interruption. Female employment has grown the fastest in economies and industries, such as retail sales, that require large numbers of interchangeable people with general rather than firm-specific or job-specific skills. But even the service sector is not a silver bullet for gender equality, because client or personnel contact and continuity are important in the highest-paying service jobs. Just as women ended up in the lowest paid assembly-line jobs in manufacturing, they tend to concentrate in the lowest paid jobs in services.

The grim implication is that women are trapped in a feedback loop. As long as women are the primary caregivers at home, employers factor the greater likelihood of their quitting or slowing down into their wages and other opportunities for advancement. But as long as a woman makes lower wages, her family will likely assign lower priority to her career rather than hamper the higher-earning family member.

One way out of this trap is for governments to push employers to treat men and women equally, regardless of the economic cost of doing so. But equal employment opportunity (EEO) legislation can never achieve perfect equality as firms have ways to disguise discrimination, and mandating parental leave has the potential to make matters even worse for women by making it more costly for firms to employ them in the first place. So far, the most extensive experiment in female employment without regard to the cost of career interruption has occurred in Scandinavian countries, not by private sector firms (which disfavor women as effectively as firms anywhere else) but by governments, which employ women in public sector jobs. Governments, of course, can do this irrespective of cost because they do not face market competition. Their challenge is instead is to convince voters that socializing the costs of family work for the sake of gender equality (or for the higher rates of fertility needed to finance social security in the future) is worth the taxpayers' expense. So far, a majority of citizens in the Scandinavian countries have agreed.

But the only way to give women an equal chance at private sector jobs is to even out the cost to employers. This means changing norms and practices so that men and women are likely to take off equal amounts of time for child rearing and other family work. It is hard to see how this could happen without strong policy intervention in the form of government subsidies covering firms' costs of hiring women, or mandating equal parental leave for both men and women. (But trying to penalize male workers who do not share equally in child care leave may just reduce fertility, if it did not fail in lawsuits first.) No country has yet moved decisively in this direction, and the best paying and most challenging private sector jobs remain starkly gender segregated.

Still, gender inequality is not inevitable. It is the social codification of economically efficient roles, and fortunately for women, what is economically efficient has become more gender-equal in the last fifty years. But we have also seen that market solutions have their limits, and the service sector may have done as much as it can to advance gender equality. It would be pleasing to suppose that gender equality marches ever onward, but history provides no grounds for such optimism. Given the importance of public policy to take gender equality to the next step—that is, to equalize the costs of family work—it is important to look at women's participation in legislative politics.

The percentage of women in national legislatures has strangely little relation to other measures of gender equality in a society, such as the gender wage gap or gender norms. This puts a sharp point on our warning that gender equality is not simply awaiting an attitude transformation. But there is another pattern underlying differences in female legislative representation. As in other labor markets, women do well in politics where career interruption is not costly. Where parties are comparatively strong and politicians are more or less interchangeable representatives of a party platform (as in the proportional representation countries of Europe), female legislative representation tends to be upwards of 30 percent—a few cases have reached virtual parity. Where parties are weak and politicians survive elections by establishing personal visibility and credibility as legislative players—often by establishing seniority in the legislative hierarchy—women do poorly. The United States illustrates this pattern: despite one of the highest female labor force participation rates in the world and a larger percentage of women in corporate management positions than any European country, the United States has a Congress that is only 12 percent female. We can show that this pattern reflects differences in constraints, rather than some strange cultural attribute, by looking at differences within countries. In the United States, the same voters who overwhelmingly choose male politicians for national office elect women to almost 30 percent of local and state offices. The reason: higher turnover at the local level makes seniority less valuable and career interruption less relevant. This same pattern can be seen in countries that combine party lists and single-member districts. In Japan, Germany, Italy, and New Zealand, women have a much better chance of getting elected to the party list portion of the ballot than to the district seats.

Political underrepresentation of women is thus an expression of the disadvantage women face in all high-powered careers. But female legislative parity may not be needed to implement policies that advance gender equality. There are many examples of politicians facilitating the aims of organized groups of activists without suffering public outrage as long as the public is not mobilized in opposition. Yet the challenges of building electoral coalitions in favor of greater gender equality are somewhat different in Europe and the United States. In the welfare states of continental Europe, where labor protections create barriers to female equality in the workforce, governments face predominantly male labor unions. Unions have to be convinced that leveling the playing field between men and women will not cost jobs for incumbent male workers. It is easier to do that in a growing than in a shrinking economy. In the United States, where fluid labor markets have already generated high levels of female labor force participation, women at the top of the income ladder may feel that they have more in common with the men above them than with the women below them. Class politics crosscuts gender politics more in the United States than in Europe, and this makes majority coalitions in favor of new initiatives for gender equality hard to assemble.

Still, progress in gender equality has been very significant during the past four decades in some countries, and we think others will follow suit. Even highly gender-stratified societies can change radically in a short time as economic, behavioral, and normative changes reinforce each other to produce an avalanche. The rise of the postindustrial economy has improved women's opportunities in the labor market, raised divorce rates, and transformed gender norms. The interaction of these changes will cause significant pressure on public policies to change as well. One sign of the pent-up demand for change is the current fertility crisis in the countries with the lowest female labor force participation rates. When traditional policies force them to choose, women are sacrificing family for careers, and it seems increasingly unlikely that norms in these countries will move back into line with policies rather than the other way around.

Women have come a long way, but they have not arrived. The challenge for future champions of women's equality is to find ways to build coalitions for progressive change that take account of evolving family, workplace, and political bargains that structure politics, employment, and domestic life.

ACKNOWLEDGMENTS

Without the help of a great number of people we could not have written this book. We have received many helpful comments and suggestions (and sometimes corrections) from Julia Adams, John Ahlquist, Jim Alt, Ben Ansell, Lucy Barnes, Rae Blumberg, Carles Boix, Richard Bribiescas, Mary Brinton, David Buss, (late) Thomas Casey, Rafaela Dancygier, Margarita Estévez-Abe, John Ferejohn, Nancy Folbre, Miriam Golden, Ben Goodrich, Michael Graetz, Kristin Hawkes, Keiko Hirao, Mata Htun, Andrea Katz, Robert Keohane, Stephen Kosack, Edward Leamer, Cathy Jo Martin, Natsu Matsuda, Nazneen Mehta, Pippa Norris, Mark Ramseyer, Nirmala Ravishankar, John Roemer, Jun Saito, Rob Salmond, Leonard Schoppa, Jim Scott, Ian Shapiro, David Soskice, John Stephens, Michael Thies, (late) Michael Wallerstein, Bruce Western, Elisabeth Wood, Anne Wren, Karen Wynn, and Vineeta Yadav and many others with whom we have had helpful conversations on this subject. We are particularly grateful to Margaret Levi and our designated commentators, John Ahlquist, Shelly Lundberg, Becky Pettit, and Blaine Robbins for their guidance when we presented an early version of the book manuscript at the University of Washington, Seattle.

1

A POLITICAL ECONOMY APPROACH
TO GENDER INEQUALITY

For thousands of years, in most of the world's societies, women have had fewer life chances than men. Certainly they have been under-represented in the ranks of the rich and powerful. But even among ordinary folk, women have been subordinated to their fathers and husbands, and sometimes to brothers and grown sons. Even in the twenty-first century, men still dominate, if to a lesser extent. Patriarchy is so much a part of life that for many people it is largely invisible. This book takes male dominance as a puzzle to be examined.

Its sheer ubiquity among many different cultures and levels of economic development has convinced many scholars that patriarchy is simply a part of human nature, whether that nature's source is evolutionary or divine. But although patriarchy has ancient roots, it has varied considerably across time and place. Male dominance was much less pronounced in hunting and gathering communities before the Neolithic Revolution, and today young women in countries as diverse as the United States and Sweden look at the subordination of their grandmothers with bewilderment. A huge variety of factors has shaped this variation, ranging from biology to culture to changing economic and political arrangements. Historians and social scientists have illuminated different dimensions of them, but none has paid sufficient attention to the ways in which these arrangements interact with the domestic dynamics between women and men. That is our focus here.

We believe the standard tools of political economy can help to explain why patriarchy is so common. It is not an inevitable part of our evolutionary heritage, like language acquisition or an omnivorous diet, but is instead a product of specific economic conditions that are nonetheless very widespread.[1] Existing social science on the family and gender relations tends to divide into two broad methodological traditions. One is rooted in a macrosociological approach that looks at how the organization of political, economic, and social institutions shapes ideologies and affects men and women differently in terms of income, careers, and political power. Esping-Andersen (1999), for example, attributes gender inequality to the institutions of the welfare state and the role of markets in the provision of services.[2] The large feminist literature on gender and the political economy traces macrolevel effects all the way down to the individual, where internalized social norms can create constrained preferences.[3] The other approach is a microeconomic analysis of how the division of household labor, fertility choices, and consumption patterns arise from considerations of household efficiency or as the result of bargaining within the family.[4] Both approaches provide valuable insights into gender inequality and family policy, but they are limited by the focus on either macro- or microlevel processes, and by their relative neglect of each other. In this book we seek a systematic integration of the two perspectives by embedding a microlevel household bargaining model in a macrolevel mode of production framework. In this embedded bargaining model the balance of power between the sexes inside the household is shaped by macrolevel conditions that define "outside options" in the event of marital dissolution.[5] Because the relevant macrolevel conditions vary across time and space, so does the power of men and women in household bargaining. Who does the laundry, who decides where to spend the family vacation, how to spend income, and so on, are all shaped by the organization of the economy and the political system, so we need a model that pays attention to macrolevel institutions and processes. This includes cultural values in the sense that equilibria in the embedded bargaining game come with common knowledge about appropriate behavior. Such common knowledge is what we usually refer to as norms, and these can take on an independent causal force in situations where there are multiple equilibria.

But it is insufficient to say that macroconditions shape household bargaining since the microdecisions by household members in turn have significant implications for macro-outcomes. When some women decide to enter into paid employment in spite of the attending social opprobrium— whether to achieve greater economic independence, improve their influ- ence over household decisions, or as an insurance against divorce—they change the incentives of other women to do the same. Because of the ex- ternalities of individual decisions, once changes have been set in motion among some women they can cause a cascade of behavioral changes that shifts the macrolevel equilibrium and alters the division of labor, public policies, and even gender norms. In this book we therefore seek to ex- plore the macroimplications of microdecisions, even as we try to under- stand how the microchoices are shaped by macroconditions. In this sense our ambition is to provide a general equilibrium model of the household where distinct family structures and gender norms are complements to distinct modes of production and political systems.

The embedded bargaining model, we suggest, can help make sense of many puzzling facts that are at the center of much comparative work on the family and political economy. One is the surprising speed of change in patriarchal norms, which philosophers and social scientists for centuries assumed to be immutable. Within just one generation a majority of girls in countries as different as the United States, Spain, and Sweden are brought up to have completely different expectations about their role in life than their mothers, or certainly their grandmothers. Reflecting the depth of this change, fifty years ago women were a rarity in higher educa- tion; today they outnumber men in many, perhaps most, Western coun- tries. From the perspective of our embedded bargaining model, this transformation marks a shift to a new equilibrium with wide-ranging im- plications for the economy, gender equality, divorce, partisan politics, and gender norms.

To illustrate this shift in terms of norms, think of values that validate fe- male subordination as a collective giving up on the possibility of female economic independence. When parents know that there is limited market demand for their daughter's labor, they will be more likely to feel obliged to equip her with attributes that give her every advantage in the marriage market instead. But rarely do parents—let alone their daughters—have to behave strategically in any conscious way, because social norms have a ten- dency to consolidate around economically efficient outcomes, and people internalize those norms unobtrusively. In game-theoretic terms such norms are equivalent to common knowledge about appropriate behavior. In many societies, girls are never taught why they must be docile, demure, and sexually chaste. They only learn that this behavior is proper, decent, and morally correct. They are rewarded for engaging in it and punished for deviating from it. But when economic autonomy becomes not only a possibility but increasingly also a necessity in a world where divorce is an ever-present concern, caring parents will teach their daughters the value of education, careers, and independence. Without having to think twice, girls brought up with these values will now tell you that an active life outside the family is the most natural thing for a woman. In chapter 2 we develop this argument further and show how rapid and fundamental changes in norms are possible when changes in macrolevel conditions set in motion microlevel choices that have large externalities. We also explain how gender norms can be understood as complements to particular modes of production.

Related to changes in gender roles is the rise in the gender gap in voting behavior that has been recorded during the past few decades. Whereas forty years ago women everywhere had political attitudes that tended to be more conservative than those of men, today the pattern is reversed in many, though not all, countries. How can we explain this shift in political preferences, and why are there countries where it has not happened? We think the answer lies in the interaction of bargaining within the household and changing macrolevel conditions. We also seek to explain why women in a country like the United States continue to be vastly underrepresented in the political arena even as they have made major inroads into the labor market and even as they seek different policies than men. This is particularly puzzling in a comparative perspective because in countries as diverse as Spain and Sweden women have reached virtual parity with men in political representation yet underperform American women in terms of gaining access to high-powered private sector jobs. Again, we think, the explanation lies in the manner macrolevel conditions—in this case political institutions—interact with microlevel decisions in the household.

Another central puzzle we seek to explain is the fact that women in countries as different as Italy and Japan are no longer having enough children to reproduce the population. This "fertility crisis" has potentially dire consequences for the future funding of the welfare state, and it cannot be disentangled from difficult political questions concerning reforms of pension systems and even whether to allow more immigration. A straightforward explanation would be that women are now having careers instead of children—a view that is popular on the religious right. But while the relationship between female labor force participation and fertility was unambiguously negative thirty years ago, today it is positive: countries where women spend a lot of time in the household tend to have lower fertility rates than countries where women are very active in the labor market. Our contention is that the explanation for the fertility crisis flows from the same underlying logic as the explanation for the political underrepresentation of women or the shift in gender norms.

In the chapters that follow, we attempt to show how these and other puzzling facts can be accounted for within the same embedded bargaining framework, integrating micro- and macrologics from the existing literature. But our ultimate aim is not to promote a particular political economy approach to the study of the family and gender relations. It is to understand why inequality in all its many facets has such a strong gender dimension, and why and how this millennium-old fact may finally be changing in a fundamental way.

Family Bargaining, Work, and Political Representation

Given the predominance of agricultural production in human history, it is not surprising that patriarchy—which imbues a stark economic division of labor with moral imperative—has been similarly entrenched in human experience. The fact that patriarchy was looser in hunter-gatherer societies, and is once again losing ground, is evidence that material causes rather than immutable human hardwiring are responsible for this otherwise exceedingly widespread form of social organization.

In modern societies, too, outside options influence bargaining within the family. We find from survey data that women with better outside options—in the form of education and job opportunities—do relatively less housework than women who lack those options, even when we control for actual hours of paid work and market income. It is a given, of course, that stay-at-home women do more housework than those who work outside the home. But we have found that a woman is able to pass off more housework onto her husband if there is merely the *possibility* of her working outside the home, as indicated by her education and by the demand for female labor in the marketplace.

Industrialization reduces the productivity advantage of male labor, but the modern welfare state hits women with an unanticipated disadvantage. Among industrial economies, the more interventionist welfare states protect workers from easy layoffs. Employers invest in their workers' firm-specific skills and naturally want to maximize their returns. They want to avoid investing in people who will then leave, taking their accumulated human capital with them. But women are left out of this game because employers know they are more likely than men to interrupt their careers for childbearing and other family work. This reduces firms' prospects of making good on long-term investments in women's human capital, and private sector firms in countries with robust labor protections thus tend to avoid hiring and promoting women. Although this dampening of female labor force participation is surely inadvertent, in most countries—in fact, in almost all of Europe outside Scandinavia as well as East Asia—it remains unaddressed.

The market economies with the least interventionist governments are, paradoxically, the most congenial to female employment. Where labor markets are relatively unprotected, a worker's expected tenure at any given firm is correspondingly short. Workers invest in general skills that are transferable across firms, and employers structure production around a fungible workforce. They do not invest extensively in worker training and so do not worry that such training would go to waste on a woman who quits to raise a family. In economies where men are as insecure in their jobs as women, the playing field is more or less gender-neutral, and family bargaining tends to be relatively egalitarian. There are, of course, trade-offs: gender equality often comes at the cost of income inequality.

The possibility of divorce also shapes the bargaining environment in the family. Women are more likely to work—and likely to do less household work—in countries with higher divorce rates. The opposite is true in countries where legal or social barriers to divorce make it difficult to take outside options, even if they exist. Where partners are forced to treat the union as a going concern, bargaining—and the division of family labor—may reflect old social norms more than would be warranted by relative levels of male and female labor productivity alone.

Domestic bargaining also affects such family decisions as how many children to have. All else being equal (and of course all else is not strictly equal since people have children for myriad reasons), as higher market demand for female labor increases women's options for remunerative work outside the home, fertility is correspondingly lower. But here we find a striking anomaly: among rich democracies, fertility is relatively high in countries with the highest female labor force participation. Apparently the opportunity cost story provides only a partial account.

Our bargaining logic unravels the puzzle. In countries with high divorce rates, women are willing to have children only if doing so does not damage their ability to earn income on their own, should the need arise. Countries with a high demand for female labor—either because of fluid private sector labor markets that do not discriminate against women or because of large public sector employment of women—provide would-be mothers with the greatest opportunity for combining family with continuous work.

Fertility is lowest of all in countries, such as Japan and Italy, with low demand for female labor and high divorce barriers—the conditions least conducive to female bargaining clout. One might expect women in these circumstances to give up on the possibility of autonomy and embrace the traditional maternal role. Perhaps because of the diffusion of values from more feminist countries, these women instead have fewer children. It is as if they are trying to eke out whatever economic independence they can. A vexing question for governments confronting this kind of fertility "strike"—some of them ironically in countries with a strong Catholic Church—is whether they need to embrace major reforms in family and labor market policies to address what is widely regarded as an emerging funding crisis for the welfare state. Much may depend on the willingness of women to abandon their embrace of policies designed to guarantee the security of the male breadwinner. If they do, the convergence of fiscal and electoral incentives may at long last compel governments everywhere to unleash the economic potential of women. This brings us to the emerging gender gap.

The Gender Gap in Democratic Politics

Government policy can influence how easily women straddle their household and market roles, both by subsidizing child care and other family work and by employing women in the public sector. The bargaining model predicts that men and women will have different preferences over these policies since they will place some value on cultivating their respective outside options apart from maximizing family income. When we tested this proposition empirically, we found that women are systematically more supportive of government spending on services and employment than men in the same income bracket. This result accounts for the gender voting gap in developed countries, where women are now more likely than men to vote for candidates and parties on the left.

A cultural theory of societal value change might predict that the gender voting gap would disappear with the crumbling of patriarchy. Instead we find that the difference between male and female preferences is largest in the most gender-equal countries. This is in fact what the bargaining model would predict. Women in countries with a strong demand for female labor are more likely to have preferences on public policy that are distinct from their husbands' than women in countries with low female labor force participation. It makes sense in a bargaining context that women would favor policies that help them improve their outside options, while men should favor the opposite. Strikingly, however, we do not find a greater gender gap in countries with more gender inequality. To the contrary, in those societies where women are in the most subordinate position in the economy and in the family, they are least likely to deviate from their husbands even when the political system allows them to do so. This is one of the puzzles we seek to solve in this book.

There is another empirical puzzle as well: the absence of a correlation between the gender voting gap—or any other measure of societal feminism—and female political representation. Countries with larger gender voting gaps do not, on average, have more female politicians. Although the female labor force participation is associated with a rise in the proportion of legislative seats going to female politicians, the effect is strongly contingent on the electoral rules. Proportional representation systems, which pit parties against each other at the national or regional level, have more female politicians than plurality systems, in which individual candidates compete for a single seat in geographic districts. Why this happens requires some exploration, since electoral rules were chosen before female political representation was permitted and so cannot have been designed with that in mind.

If we think about the market for politicians in the same terms as other labor markets, we can see how electoral rules that place a premium on career continuity can create a bias against female success. The political market acts much like a labor market with long-term contracts, which creates statistical discrimination against women through the expectation of career interruptions for family reasons. District-based systems, particularly those that require politicians to establish strong personal reputations, favor politicians who can accumulate political capital over a long career. As long as mothers are the default caretakers of children, women politicians will compete at a disadvantage against men, who can begin their careers early and stick with the job. Voters need have no predisposition against women for this disadvantage to exist, and indeed, female candidates who pass the nomination hurdles tend to do as well as men. But because of past career interruptions, relatively few women can match the political capital of men at any given stage in their careers.

In proportional electoral systems, by contrast, each party presents voters with a slate of candidates who represent the party's collective face. Because parties compete with each other on programmatic grounds, attention centers on the policies each party advocates rather than on the personal qualities or political clout of individual candidates. Female politicians do not confront high barriers to advancement in this system because time spent on family work does not interfere with acquiring the qualities that win politicians a place on the list: loyalty to the party platform and the ability to articulate the party's priorities. Qualification for higher office does not depend on seniority and the accumulation of personal political capital. The exceptions are the top leadership posts, which as in the district-based systems require accumulated experience, networks, and bargaining credibility. Even for these positions, however, women often have a better chance than in majoritarian systems because the pool of experienced female politicians is larger, and because the party continues to play a greater role in policy formation and competition for voters.[6]

Several kinds of evidence favor this explanation over the alternative, that there exists a cultural bias against women in politics. In addition to the cross-national comparisons in which proportional representation systems send more women into politics, we observe that in countries with mixed systems, women are more likely to be elected on lists than from districts. When countries switch electoral rules from proportional representation to districts, female representation declines, and it increases when they switch in the other direction. Another piece of evidence against a cultural explanation is that women do simultaneously better in business and worse in politics in the United States, with its district-based system, than in most countries with proportional representation. Clearly the cross-country comparisons are not merely picking up some national level of gender stereotyping.

Children in the Family Bargain

Our model poses a challenge to the traditional economic analysis of the family, in which the family is a unitary actor maximizing a single utility function: the family's overall well-being. The false power of that assumption becomes apparent when we see how many of the standard conclusions fall away when it is altered. A woman's individual utility may be lowered under a division of labor that maximizes family income if she has no control over the money's allocation. It is also lowered if she takes on all household duties and neglects developing her marketable skills, because marketable skills are the only ones she can use if the marriage dissolves. The problem is particularly severe for time spent on children, because this is a specific investment that carries no value in the remarriage market. Alternatively, a man may become worse off when his wife goes into the labor market and raises total family income if her enhanced bargaining power reduces his slice of an enlarged pie or if he now has less time for developing his own marketable skills.

Note that there is no implication here that people have children for purely economic reasons. That may have been approximately true in agricultural societies when children were an indispensable source of labor and insurance in old age. In postindustrial societies children tend to be a net cost that is outweighted only by deep-seated desires for love, companionship, and procreation. Rational choice theory does not explain such desires, and nor do we. Our argument about fertility is instead that the desire to have children comes at a cost that differs across countries. The severity of the trade-off determines the extent to which women sacrifice children for careers. Rational choice theory *can* help us understand choices in this trade-off.

In fairness to the efficiency model, it is important to remember that the family is taken to be maximizing collective utility, including that of children, rather than income per se. It makes more sense to us to extend the model to include the utility of children rather than to subsume them into a family unit. What's best for the children may not be best for the parents, and vice versa.

The idea that child care, at least during some stages of the child's life, cannot be subcontracted out of the family without some loss of utility for the child rests on assumptions that remain contested among experts.[7] We will not weigh in on that debate, except to note that attachment parenting does not require that the mother be the principal caregiver. We focus instead on the parents' asymmetrical accumulation of marketable skills and experience. Even if the children are better off having a parent at home for some period, this benefit comes at some cost to a parent who, in order to provide it, abstains from investing in the labor market. The fact that it is difficult for the mother to exclude her husband from benefiting from her investment in the children—assuming both parents delight in healthy and well-adapted children—further undermines her bargaining position.[8]

This trade-off shows up in a striking tendency for women in some countries to have fewer children. What is sometimes called a fertility crisis has its source, we argue, in women's increasing desire for financial independence from men. If marketable skills are the only insurance against the consequences of divorce, and if child care is too expensive or hard to find, women will sacrifice large families to build sustainable careers. The fertility crisis is perhaps the most vivid manifestation of the conflict between men and women over the division of labor. Efficiency arguments not only fail to explain this phenomenon but blind us to the efficiency consequences of gender conflict. As the Scandinavians realized when they faced their own fertility crisis, the funding of the welfare state, especially pensions and healthcare for older people, depends crucially on a large, economically active younger generation. Efficiency, in the broader sense of intergenerational sustainability, cannot be separated from the question of how to manage distributive conflict between the sexes.

Efficiency does not, then, capture all the dimensions of the problem we care about. But it nonetheless remains an important concept for the political economy of gender. We have noted that social norms about gender roles tend to solidify around the efficient allocation of family resources regardless of the distributional effects on family members. In agricultural societies, which historically made up the vast bulk of human communities, male physical strength was put to productive use in tilling the land while women were fully employed in the home, keeping offspring alive under formidable conditions. Economic efficiency is thus one of the drivers of patriarchy.

It has been objected that efficiency is itself a creation of the male mind and has been used as a tool of domination.[9] What better way to get the entire female sex to submit to male rule than to persuade them it was for the common good? As modern social scientists, we endanger the objectivity of our enterprise if we buy into an ideology that has enslaved women and other weak groups for millennia.

While we do not doubt that patriarchs have enjoyed their dominance within the family or that many have used brute force to defend it, male power cannot be the whole causal story, as some would have it. Men face enormous problems acting collectively to achieve any common purpose. These problems are compounded by their competition for desirable female mates. Given the uneven allocation of strength among males and their competing interests, male collusion should be extraordinarily precarious. Although polygamy is a terrible system for men at the bottom of the ladder, monogamy is unstable under conditions of unequal wealth when wealthy men compete for the most desirable women. Male power alone cannot account for variation in family forms or for vertical power structures.

An explanation of patriarchy requires elements of both power and efficiency. Over the many centuries since the Neolithic Revolution, people and societies have competed for land and other resources. Competition rewards the productive allocation of assets and punishes the less productive with annihilation or abandonment. Efficient allocation of resources changes with the technology of production, but for much of human history, agricultural production has favored male physical strength and child survival has favored female nurturing.[10]

Among families and across communities, a wide variety of factors created winners and losers. Societies waxed and waned. Our account concerns what happened within families in all of those places. Agricultural production everywhere favored male brawn, and the exigencies of survival forced considerable homogeneity around a division of labor that left men dominant over and thus better off than women. Social norms validated this strategy, sparing each new generation costly errors. Male power is as much consequence as cause.

Gender and Domestic Bargaining

The embedded bargaining model of gender incorporates important insights from the three dominant social science paradigms that have been applied to account for patriarchy: materialism, institutionalism, and explanations that focus on values and beliefs. *Materialism* encompasses a wide category of arguments, but they all have two things in common: the primacy of material resources in generating effective demands on government, and the material basis of the interests imputed to groups of people who possess those resources.[11] Our approach shares a strong focus on modes of production and material interests, but we pay more attention to institutional design and conditions outside the market than is common in this literature. Household bargaining and decisions interact with market conditions as well as political and economic institutions that cannot be captured by a simple state versus market dichotomy.

Institutionalism involves a similarly broad collection of theories regarding government and market institutions and the relations among them. Institutions are important in our analysis because they are part of the environment in which individual bargaining is embedded. But while institutions shape behavior, they are occasionally also transformed by such behavior. The massive inflow of women into the labor market has unquestionably had consequences for the workings of both economic institutions and the welfare state, and we seek to understand these effects as well. Rather than treating institutions as immutable exogenous constraints on behavior, we view them as endogenous to equilibria that are also shaped by behavior.

The third paradigm takes *ideas and values* to be autonomous from both institutions and resources. We agree that, in the short and medium run, values are very powerful. But in the longer run, material forces shape both institutions and values. Changes in production technology, in our argument, drive the emergence and demise of patriarchy by giving and then taking away a productivity advantage to male labor. Competition over resources in societies with labor-intensive agriculture creates patriarchal family institutions.[12] Social norms are principally a result rather than a cause of patriarchy: families socialize their children in ways that help them navigate the strategic environment they will face. This is not to deny that for any relatively short period of time, norms can be powerful autonomous forces that are thoroughly internalized, invisible, and resistant to change. In the countries now suffering a fertility crisis, for example, new opportunities for women in the labor markets have clearly shifted the balance of power toward a less gender-divided division of labor, but traditional norms seem to have blocked any effective political solution. If we are right that norms ultimately adapt to economic necessity, those countries will see profound changes in family policy over the next decade or so. We believe this is precisely what is happening in a country like Spain where traditional values represented by the Catholic Church are challenged by economic and political change. Perhaps other countries with similar patriarchial institutions and traditions are not far behind.

The many variants of the institutionalist paradigm take the organization of political and economic incentives as crucial in shaping the demand for policies. It stands to reason that the incentive structures of legislatures would reflect the markets they regulate, and vice versa. Countries with proportional representation (PR) electoral rules are more likely to have strong labor parties that can gain labor protections and set the stage for long-term labor contracts. PR also facilitates consensus-based regulatory institutions that manage and implement these rules, as well as those governing skill formation and wage-setting.[13] In majoritarian and district-based systems, parties compete with each other to keep taxes low and markets fluid, and consensus-building is inhibited.

The market institutions that map onto each type of electoral system, in turn, profoundly affect the productivity of male versus female labor. In labor markets characterized by long-term contracts, women are a bad investment, as we have seen. Proportional representation and long-term labor contracts were not adopted with the intent of suppressing women's market power, but they will not disappear once voters become aware of this effect. It is very difficult to change economic institutions that benefit incumbent workers. On the other hand, PR electoral systems have facilitated the political representation of women and their interests, which has modified the operation of labor markets.

We need all three paradigms, then, to make sense of the relative bargaining leverage of men and women. Which variants of materialist accounts are most useful depends on how production technology and the regulatory environment affect various actors' ability to take collective action. In today's rich democracies, women's interests are poorly aligned with class because it is a very heterogeneous group and because labor parties are organized to protect existing—predominantly male—workers.[14] More generally, whether resources, institutions, or values are causes or consequences depends on where one slices into the story and how long a perspective on history one takes. In the long run, technological change and modes of production loom large. In the medium run, institutions, and in the short run, also norms become much more prominent.

Conclusions

Historical and cultural differences in the degree and style of male dominance provide intriguing clues as to why and how men have ruled the world for so long. The productivity of male versus female labor, depending on modes of production, provides a baseline explanation. In hunter-gatherer societies, the division of labor between male hunting and female gathering did not remove women from a source of their own food, should they seek to dissolve a relationship with a male partner.

The Neolithic Revolution was also a patriarchal revolution because sedentary agriculture and herding shifted the advantage of food production to male brawn and consigned women to a supplementary and family-centered role. Women lost their social mobility when their family-specific investments in children took away their economic viability outside the family unit. By contrast, a man controlled resources with which he could dominate his family and also cultivate other relationships. The possibility of storing food, trading it in the marketplace, and conquering others' stores makes agricultural societies considerably more complex than hunter-gatherer ones, opening up new levels of wealth, social hierarchy, and military organization. These in turn increased the importance of the marriage market for women and the strategic value of teaching daughters how to "marry up." The resulting web of gendered role expectations is patriarchal in the extreme.

Social norms grew up around agricultural economies but survived into the industrial age, despite a gradual decline in the productivity advantage of male brawn. This is partly because of the stickiness of values. Even if a woman could operate a big machine, the idea was anathema to the Victorians who both introduced machines to the world and did their best to keep women, petticoats and all, well away from them.

Eventually, the increased demand for female labor in postindustrial societies and the need for more family income would inspire many women to push past the bars of the domestic cage. Once they did, an irreversible process of change was set in motion by the accumulation of hundreds and thousands of individual decisions, which in turn affected the decisions of millions of others. But electoral rules, and the market arrangements they both reflect and reinforce, generate vastly different levels of demand for female labor. Only Scandinavia has brought women into the labor force in numbers comparable to men—partly on account of a more flexible labor market, but mostly by hiring them into public sector service jobs. In market-based economies like the United States, women have also made significant inroads into the private labor market, but they have been left at a huge disadvantage in the political system.

The embedded bargaining model of gender follows the fall and rise of women's economic autonomy through the ages. In modern democracies, the power of public policy to bend markets to public priorities creates new opportunities to address the concerns of women left behind in the march to equality. Explaining why those policies are needed is the purpose of this book.

2

THE STRUCTURE OF PATRIARCHY: HOW BARGAINING POWER SHAPES SOCIAL NORMS AND POLITICAL ATTITUDES

As a natural consequence of our division of labor on sex-lines, giving to woman the home and to man the world in which to work, we have come to a dense prejudice in favor of the essential womanliness of the home duties.

—Charlotte Perkins Gilman, *Women and Economics*, 1898, p. 111

Patriarchy—the dominance of males in social, economic, and political organization—characterizes much of human history. If Mr. Cleaver from the 1950s in America were to time-travel back to an ancient agricultural village, he would, after the initial shock, take comfort in the stereotypical roles of the male household head who rules over his wife and children. Even Mrs. Cleaver, in the subordinate role, would find her status in that ancient society familiar. Then as now, the variance in gender norms across societies remains within recognizable bounds.

Patriarchy's very universality has made it invisible to otherwise perceptive philosophers and social critics from ages past. Jean-Jacques Rousseau, an early modern champion of equality, applied his logic only to men. Not only did Rousseau fail to argue for gender equality, but as Nannerl Keohane has pointed out, he elevated the power differential between men and women "into a 'moral' principle that becomes the foundation of an immense and complicated argument about how men and women should behave in all aspects of their lives."[1] Rousseau, of course, was validating an ancient belief rather than devising a new one. From the beginning of recorded history, men have not only been dominant, but societies have held that it is right that they should be so. The heavens smile, the cosmos is balanced, God is pleased. We single out Rousseau not because he was unusually chauvinistic.[2] Our point is rather that his disparaging attitude toward women was so utterly common that this champion of equality mistook convention for natural law, as a long line of fellow men had done before him.

Patriarchal conventions, or the social norms that make common sense of male dominance, have assigned women to second-class citizenship for millennia. Because these norms have been with us for so long, this chapter takes our focus far back in time to understand where they came from and why they are both ubiquitous and persistent. The answer that emerges is not about how men have tricked women into subservience. Rather, patriarchal norms have tracked economically efficient uses of human resources, creating a bigger economic pie than in their absence. But they also reflect unequal power between the genders because at the Pareto frontier men have a bargaining advantage that derives from their ability to leave the household more easily.

Economically efficient organization of productive resources can have starkly inegalitarian consequences, as epitomized by labor-intensive agriculture.[3] The premium to male brawn in agricultural economies encourages a gendered specialization of labor that gives males command over assets that are more mobile than the female's family-specific investments. Regardless of the importance of the woman's contribution to the family well-being, the man is in a position to appropriate the returns of her work because his assets—his farming ability and experience—are more mobile than her family-specific investments, particularly her children.

Gender equality in human history takes on the shape of a giant U, starting with—as far as we know—relatively egalitarian hunter-gatherer societies in which females were economically self-sufficient from their gathering role, falling into a trough of inequality when females became specialized in family work in agrarian societies, and then moving into greater equality as females gained access to market opportunities for which brawn was no longer at a premium. This is a different U from the one that Friedrich

Engels drew (1985), in which markets and commodification of labor were the culprits that dragged women into slavery until communism would release them. Unlike Engels, we argue that it is not markets per se but the way particular kinds of markets encourage specialization and allocate bargaining power across the sexes that shape opportunities for gender equality.

The logic has a timeless quality, though the differences in asset mobility between men and women are sharpest in agricultural societies. Different modes of economic production shape the intrahousehold bargaining environment and, by extension, influence social norms that allocate duties and rights across the sexes. It would be ideal, from the standpoint of social science research, if we had access to information about gender norms from prehistoric times and could trace their changes through various modes of economic production and family organization. Short of that, we can examine change in norms during the limited periods of history for which we have reliable data. Because of the great disparity in levels of economic development across human societies today, we can also observe how well different economic systems correspond to the value systems that we would predict.

In this chapter, we make use of psychologists' cross-cultural research on mate selection preferences for evidence that families choose to socialize their daughters differently under different systems of economic production. We find, as we would expect, that agrarian societies have the most discernibly patriarchal values, and they put pressure on girls to play to the marriage market rather than to acquire market-relevant skills on their own. Patriarchal values begin to attenuate in industrial societies, but they tend to be far weaker in postindustrial societies.

Efficiency, Bargaining, and Patriarchy

It is tempting to think that men, on account of their strength advantage over women, have collectively written the rules of the game in their favor. From the beginning of the human race, men would have had a common interest in clamping down on any freewheeling female impulses —particularly any impulses to mate wantonly and hide information about the paternity of their offspring—and they should have been strong enough to call the shots. Especially once societies became sedentary and men had assets to bequeath to the next generation, men must have been anxious to know which children were theirs.[4]

Although there may be some truth to this account of male collusion, a collective action account based on brute strength alone fails to explain the stability of that outcome given that males compete with each other for females. Males competing with other males may use various strategies to appeal to potential female mates, of which forcible sex or female subordination more generally is only one. For one thing, males competing with one another for females should be motivated to cheat on the collective male enterprise by promising a better deal. For another, females are the choosier sex since females bear by far the larger burden from sexual reproduction than males, and female selection could well favor kind, nurturing qualities in males.[5] The stability of patriarchal values that valorize female subordination against the backdrop of male competition is more of a puzzle than one might assume.

Arguably, patriarchy—along with, perhaps, respect for authority more generally—is the most encompassing and persistent set of social conventions that has governed human society. Our contribution to this line of analysis is to consider how patriarchal norms became virtually universal and to explore the conditions under which patriarchy remains stable or begins to erode. Our argument begins with the observation that in agricultural society, households could secure efficiency gains by organizing themselves around a gendered division of labor in which males specialized in labor-intensive agriculture and females specialized in family work, including, primarily, the bearing and rearing of children.[6]

Conceptualizing Power between the Sexes

Bargaining theory implies, and casual observation confirms, that power often flows from the ability of people to walk away from a deal. This is true whether we talk about haggling over the price of a used car, bargaining over wages, or deciding the division of household labor in the family. In bargaining theory the ability to walk away is in part captured by the concept of "outside options": an agreement has to leave each bargainer at least as well off as he or she would be without an agreement. This means that outside options are constraints on the bargained outcome.

In principle, outside options do not affect the bargained outcome unless the constraint binds. But if there is a risk that negotiations will break down, the less risk-averse player will have an advantage, and it stands to reason that this player is the one with less to loose—namely, the one with better outside options. Between otherwise identical individuals, therefore, those with the better outside prospects can more credibly threaten to hold out for a better agreement unless the deal is already tilted toward them. The same result holds when one player is more "patient," which is likely to be the one who has less to fear from having no agreement.

This is not the whole story about power, because the outcome may also depend on altruism and, less easy to pin down, norms of fairness as well as the ability to manipulate or persuade others. More important, if an efficient contract involves investments that themselves affect outside options, such as a "Beckerian marriage contract" where the woman invests heavily in household-specific assets, the contract itself may depend on a credible commitment not to dissolve it (see appendix A for more detail). If contract termination is truly prohibited ("marriage till death you part"), there are no such things as outside options, and "inside options," especially the relative tolerance of living in a noncooperative marriage, become decisive. In reality, rules against marriage dissolution have rarely prevented males from de facto abandoning a wife if alternatives are sufficiently attractive, so we are likely to learn a great deal about power, especially over long stretches of historical time, if we can identify variables that affect the relative ability of people in a bargaining relationship to prosper if they abandon it. Norms against marriage dissolution, however, are part of our story because we should expect these to become more salient if women are unlikely to enter marriage—and accept all the duties that come with it—unless they have some insurance against dissolution.

In modern times, the obvious equivalent of "walking away" from a family is divorce, and much recent scholarship in fact centers on that notion.[7] But marriage is not a precondition for forming households, nor is divorce the only way to walk away from a marriage. In hunter-gatherer societies, men and women formed households, or families, but they did not get married in the modern meaning of the term. Still, they were clearly in a bargaining relationship. In agricultural societies marriage became ubiquitous, and the norm against divorce was strong. Nevertheless, it was common for men to withdraw from their family responsibilities, not merely through infidelity and diversion of time and resources, but sometimes by altogether leaving the family to its own devices, physically and economically.

The ability to walk away in this sense depends critically on having skills and assets that can be applied easily outside the household. If all of one's assets are tied to the household, the loss of leaving can be prohibitive. In agricultural societies, as we have argued, physical capacity for hard labor is an asset that can be applied outside the household as well as inside it, whereas investments in children are specific to the household. This is true certainly until children are old enough to work for others. Children also impose a cost on women in the remarriage market in that another man's children do not provide the same psychic benefit as one's own offspring.

Aside from outside options, leaving or neglecting the family also means that any household-specific investment will be lost, or at least seriously devalued. Whatever time and money the male has spent on the family in the past is not likely to yield much of a return in the future unless he remains in the household. To the extent that children's economic or emotional stability requires continuous investment through a certain age, the departure of their father prior to that age reduces all previous investment in their well-being.[8]

We conjecture that men's outside options have been greater than women's throughout much of history because women, by most accounts, have a *comparative* advantage (though not necessarily an *absolute* advantage) in household-specific assets, and men have a *comparative* advantage in physical capacity for hard labor, and the skills that come from engaging in such labor, which are a mobile asset. When the production technology, or mode of production, generates high demand for physical labor and a premium on having many children, as in agricultural societies, the gain from having a more or less complete division of labor is high and bargaining power will heavily advantage the male. But there is no reason that either sex should have a comparative advantage in mobile assets that require little or no hard physical labor, such as social and intellectual skills that are used intensely in most service production. The gain from a complete division of labor in the household will therefore be smaller, and women will have a reason to avoid it precisely because specialization for women means less power over outcomes.[9] The result is that the outside options of women improve, and men consequently have a smaller bargaining advantage. Since the efficiency gains from specialization are lower, bargaining considerations will become more salient in determining the division of labor.

There is an important knock-on effect of a less complete division of labor, which is that the gains from marriage diminish. As the outside options of women improve, the bargaining space, or marital surplus, diminishes. If other factors that influence the marital surplus—such as emotional attachment, compatibility of personalities, consumption preferences, tolerance for disagreement, and so on—vary in ways that are in the aggregate random, the probability that the sum of outside options exceeds the value of the marriage will go up. This in turn increases the incidence of divorce and expands the size of the remarriage market. When this happens the opportunities outside the marriage improve, and the incentives of the spouses to work to cultivate their outside options also increase, which reduce the division of labor, and so on, thus moving society to a higher divorce, lower division of labor equilibrium.[10] This logic conforms to the network or strategic complementarities game that it will be useful to set out more formally in the next section. It is also true, of course, that as women become more economically independent, nonmaterial motivations for marriage such as love, companionship, and mutual respect become more important, with the result that the marriages that survive the drop in gains from specialization are likely to be stronger. But on average, higher divorce rates and higher levels of female market participation go together.

The Gender Division of Labor as a Network Game

Because the individual decisions by women to enter into paid employment affect the incentives of others to do the same, we cannot analyze these decisions in isolation. The bargaining approach to the family is extremely useful in highlighting the way socioeconomic conditions—or outside options—affect power between the sexes and hence the decisions made by each household member, but it does not account for how these decisions are aggregated to produce macrolevel outcomes. The bargaining approach is technically speaking a partial equilibrium model. Because we are ultimately interested in macrolevel outcomes, we need a general equilibrium model where the aggregation of microlevel decisions is explicit.

This is what we set out to do in this section, using the simple network game illustrated in figure 2.1.

On the y-axis is the probability of an individual woman, i, entering the labor market and hence leaving the household for at least part of the available time. On the x-axis we record the expected share of all women participating in the labor market. Assuming that individuals are identical, in equilibrium the probability of an individual woman entering the labor market must equal the share of women in the labor market. This is the 45-degree line. Because a woman's propensity to enter the labor market is affected by whether other women do the same, the decision to enter the labor market is a strategic complementarities game. There are three specific complementarities. The first is a purely economic one. As more women enter the labor market the demand for services such as day care and housekeeping will increase, and so will the demand for female labor. This facilitates working and raises the opportunity costs of not working. The second effect goes through divorce rates. As more women enter paid employment and more services are offered through the market, the gains from the gender division of labor fall. Since one of the principal gains from marriage is the division of labor, as captured by the Becker model, the probability of divorce rises as the division of labor blurs. Higher divorce rates in turn make it less desirable to invest in household-specific assets, which make entry into paid employment more desirable. We have modeled this logic elsewhere and have shown that there is a tight empirical relationship between female labor force participation and divorce rates across Organization of Economic Cooperation and Development (OECD) countries.[11] The third complementarity concerns changes in gender norms, which both follow from and reinforce divorce and labor force participation.

It is our contention that bargaining power translates into inequities between the genders that are "codified" in norms of behavior. These norms, we suggest, are amplified by the socialization behavior of caring parents who are preparing their sons and daughters for adulthood. In agricultural societies, with a stark gender division of labor and a strong bargaining advantage for men, socialization of girls will come to reflect this inequity in ways that not only maximize girls' position in the marriage market but make it easier for females to accept their subordination in the marriage. By

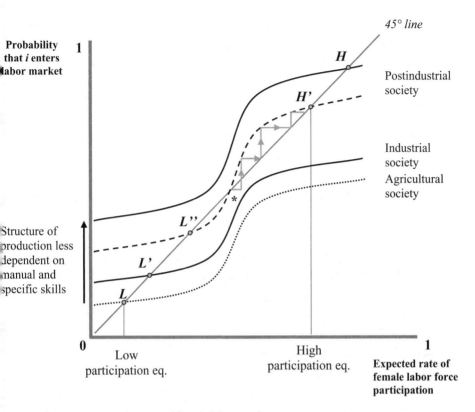

Figure 2.1. A network game of female labor market entry

the same token, our "mode of production" explanation implies that caring parents will socialize boys and girls to have more equitable gender norms as the bargaining advantage of men is eroded in the course of the transition to a service-based economy. As daughters are taught values that will help them succeed in the labor market, these females will be more likely to enter paid work when they reach adulthood.[12] As they do, more women will be drawn into the labor market, and so on. Although the effects of norm change may be delayed by the time it takes socialization to work itself through generational replacement, there are obvious network externalities of such change.

We think it is empirically and theoretically plausible to expect the probability of participation to follow the cumulative standard normal distribution, which is captured by the S-shaped relationship between (expected) female labor force participation and probability of labor market entry illustrated in figure 2.1. The logic is as follows. Starting from the left in the figure and focusing on the bottom dotted curve, even when other women are not expected to work there is some incentive for each woman i to do so. Some jobs for women will always be available, and even if divorce is not a concern and all household duties fall on the woman there are life-cycle incentives for women to participate in paid employment, entering the labor market before children are born and after they leave the household (as implied by the original Becker model). As expected levels of female labor force participation rise as a consequence, each woman's propensity to participate for purely economic reasons will also rise. But as long as the economy and labor demand favor males, women will not be able to abandon their household duties, and female participation in the labor market will consequently stop well short for that of males. This occurs where the relatively "flat" response function cuts the upward-sloping 45-degree line in figure 2.1. This low-participation equilibrium (denoted L) will be bolstered by legal and normative protections of the traditional family, which make investments in household-specific assets less risky for females. In the L equilibrium the majority of women who do not work, or who work only temporarily or part time, will depend heavily on the male breadwinner, and they will likely adopt "conservative" views on the family to reinforce norms against abandoning or otherwise endangering the sanctity of the family. The L equilibrium loosely speaking corresponds to the Becker model.[13]

If we move beyond the L equilibrium, at some point of relatively high female participation divorce rates will begin to rise and gender norms will begin change accordingly, prompting women to enter the labor market at a faster rate. Because the supply and demand for family services through the market are also rising, the opportunity costs of not participating also become considerable. This is the steep upward-sloping part of the S curve. When the probability of entering the labor market reaches a very high level, additional labor market participation by other women will again have only modest effects on the decision to enter the labor market. Some women will always choose to remain home regardless of what other women do. This is the top, flat part of the curve. Whether the top part of the curve intersects the 45-degree line, and hence enables a high participation (H) equilibrium, is ultimately an empirical question. But we can theorize about the location of the S function, and hence the equilibrium, which will depend on the mode of production.

The S curve in an agricultural economy (the bottom dotted line in figure 2.1) is likely to intersect the 45-degree line only at the low-participation L point, which is associated with a distinct bargaining disadvantage for women, even if the division of labor is efficient. Correspondingly, we would expect low divorce rates and very patriarchical gender norms in this case. With industrialization the curve shifts upward as demand for female labor outside the household increases (the bottom solid line). As a consequence more women will enter paid employment. But most will still be economically dependent on a male breadwinner, and gender norms will continue to reflect the strong bargaining position of men. While women are now in a position to supplement the income of males, thereby providing both a measure of insurance and some additional consumption, the role of women is still strictly bound by her primary duties as a mother and wife. The gender division of labor continues to be stark, and we continue to be in a low-participation equilibrium (denoted L' in figure 2.1).

Postindustrialization, in contrast, because it shifts demand away from manual labor and toward jobs requiring general skills, creates far more equitable labor market opportunities for women. This in turn opens the possibility of a high-participation equilibrium. The scenario is illustrated by the top solid curve and the associated H equilibrium in figure 2.1. Here bargaining power between the sexes will be relatively equal and the patterns of socialization and norms are correspondingly likely to be less gendered. Modern democracies have all moved toward the H equilibrium as they transition to a more service-intensive economy. But as we argue in detail in subsequent chapters, this has not eliminated gender inequality or done away with notable cross-national differences in the structure of the family. The reason, we argue, is partly that the labor market everywhere continues to favor males, especially for high-powered careers in the private sector, but it is partly also that the organization of economic institutions and partisan politics in some countries continues to support a low-participation equilibrium. The situation corresponds to the dashed S curve in figure 2.1, which intersects the 45-degree line three times, two of which represent stable equilibria (donoted L″ and H′). The middle intersection is unstable in the sense that a small disturbance, such as the slight increase in expected labor force participation indicated by an asterisk (*), will produce a chain reaction in behavior that moves the outcome to either L″ or H′. The process by which this occurs is illustrated by the arrows at the center of the figure (in this example producing an H′ equilibrium). The important point is that both L″ and H′ are sustainable equilibria, and we argue later that among currently advanced democracies, which are at similar levels of development, it is possible to observe quite distinct gender "regimes," which are tied to particular economic and political institutions (and of course gender norms).

If we try to look forward into the future it is quite possible that the L equilibrium will everywhere disappear as the S curve keeps moving upward (as illustrated by the top solid curve in figure 2.1). If and when the S curve no longer intersects the 45-degree line at the bottom end, a cascade of changes will occur in former L countries whereby women will enter the labor market in large numbers, household bargaining power will shift in favor of females, and gender norms will turn more egalitarian. This is, we believe, broadly speaking what happened in North America and Scandinavia in the 1970s, and it is something that might be occurring right now in a country like Spain where the traditional family appears to be quickly giving way to a new equilibrium with women assuming much more active roles in the economy. It is of course an intense social and political battle involving a powerful Catholic Church and a traditionalist right, but the Socialists have made a big gamble in pushing for gender equality and we would not be surprised if they are doing so at just the right time. If this happens, how far behind can other countries with a traditional gender division of labor be?

But in this chapter we mostly look back in time and provide a broadbrush interpretation of gender norms as they have developed through the longue durée of economic history. That interpretation is outlined in table 2.1 and implies a curvilinear relationship between economic development and gender equality. Historically there was a sharp rise in inequality from hunter-gatherer societies to agricultural societies, and then a gradual reduction of inequality as we move to industrial and then postindustrial societies. We do not deny, of course, that political mobilization or institutions are important. Indeed, later in this chapter and in the rest of the book we underscore their importance for understanding gender politics in modern democracies. But in the long sweep of historical time, the underlying power relationships between men and women shape institutions and values. We do not want to suggest that there are no relevant distinctions in the mode of production within each of these categories. Our argument implies that such differences will matter for gender relations and norms, and in subsequent chapters we will make more fine-grained distinctions between skill-based modern economies. But there are still broad historical trends that we believe reflect underlying forces that also differentiate contemporary political economies.

Modes of Production

Different modes of production affect intergender bargaining power, female participation in the economy, and, by extension, the evolution of social norms. Both the male and female roles may be equally vital to the survival of the family, but the relative bargaining power of the man and the woman is shaped instead by the reversion point for each in the event of family dissolution. Agrarian production generates sharp asymmetries between the sexes in life prospects upon the breakdown of a family, which should lead to pronounced differences in gender norms. These asymmetries are less pronounced in hunter-gatherer and in industrial and especially postindustrial economic systems, leading us to expect gender norms to be the most stark in agrarian societies (see table 2.1).

Hunter-Gatherer Economies

Our knowledge of hunter-gatherer systems is limited to archeological evidence and ethnographic reports of times past, and to information about a few extant hunter-gatherer societies that survive at the edges of agrarian communities in Africa, Asia, and Latin America. Given our limited knowledge, what we say about these societies is necessarily speculative. As far as we know from what paleontologists have gleaned about these societies, women seem to have had the ability to survive independently of a male provider.[14] In their book *Woman the Gatherer* (1981), Frances Dahl-

Table 2.1. Modes of production and gender inequality

		Demand for nonmanual labor	
		Low	High
Demand for hard physical labor ("brawn") and household-specific skills.	Low	Hunter-gatherer: High equality between the sexes.	Postindustrial society: High equality in bargaining power. Modest division of labor and equitable gender norms.
	High	Agricultural society: Male dominance. Sharp division of labor and patriarchal norms.	Industrial society: Sharp division of labor but emerging opportunities for women outside the family.

berg and her collaborators revised the conventional wisdom put forth in *Man the Hunter* (Lee and Devore 1968) that men provided the food, pointing out that women seem to have typically provided three-quarters or more of the daily caloric intake of the community with the tubers and other plant foods they gathered. The protein provided by men might have been particularly desirable, and men might have been able to gain status and access to women by sharing meat; but the meat was not strictly necessary for survival, especially in areas with protein-rich pulses. Moreover, because meat would have been hard to store, hierarchies among men are likely to have been relatively underdeveloped and fluid and based on hunting skill or, with population density, warrior prowess rather than on heredity.

Physical anthropologists characterize hunter-gatherer family structure as serial monogamy, in which a couple might break up at the instigation of either party and either partner may "remarry" several times in a lifetime. Divorce does not seem to be particularly discouraged or uncommon in the hunter-gatherer societies we know about, and divorce does not lead to a sharp drop in the woman's livelihood. Women share child-care duties among themselves, and grandmothers, by providing supplemental child care and food gathering, may be more important than husbands to the survival of the young.[15]

For the purposes of our bargaining model, it is important that divorce seems to have had a roughly symmetrical effect on both members of a couple in a hunter-gatherer society. The woman's livelihood and child-care arrangements would be largely unchanged, though she might have an incentive to remarry to have privileged access to meat. She continues to rely on her gathering work for nourishing herself and her children, and having existing children does not seriously damage her chances in the remarriage market because she and her circle of female kin and friends continue to bear primary responsibility for their care. Neither does the presence of these children seriously impede her ability to gather food. In this setting marriage does not provide an overwhelming economic advantage, and it is unsurprising that they often did not last.

Although this picture is somewhat idealized, the crucial point is that to the extent that women are, along with men, economically viable outside of marriage, the bargaining relationship between men and women is likely to be relatively equal within marriage, and marriage itself is a less sacred and important institution. Both partners in a relationship have investments —he in hunting, she in gathering and child care—that are more or less equally mobile across family units. Although a new husband will not likely value her children from a previous marriage, she retains the ability to provide for them and for herself across marriages.

To the extent that women are economically viable without a male patron, we expect parents to have no particular reason to socialize their daughters to behave differently from their sons, apart from the economic specialization entailed in hunter-gatherer societies. Where marriage is not necessary for livelihood, it need not last a lifetime, and parents worry less to ensure that their daughters marry the best possible mate. Because female economic autonomy puts males in a weaker position to demand the "female virtues" of virginity, chastity, and quiet subservience, we expect social norms will less likely form around these male preferences.

Agrarian Economies

Although gradual, the shift from hunter-gatherer to sedentary agriculture introduced a profound shift in the bargaining relationship within families. By extension the Neolithic Revolution set the stage for a very different set of social norms. Population growth and land scarcity increased the frequency and intensity of warfare, enhancing the value of male warriors to the community. This seems particularly to have been true where patrilocal living arrangements emerged, which possibly reinforced the male bonding deemed so important in battle but robbed women of their kinship networks.[16] Moreover, with population growth and land scarcity, cultivation of food became more labor intensive, bringing with it a premium on male brawn in plowing and other heavy farmwork. Within the family unit, an efficient division of labor utilized the man's physical strength to cultivate food, while the woman specialized in bearing and rearing children, processing and preparing food, making clothes, and other family duties—including helping in the fields when feasible. Though a woman's work was crucial to the survival of the family, her role no longer gave her economic viability on her own.

We argue that it was the loss of economic independence that gave rise to social norms that made marriage the ultimate goal for a woman, for without marriage, a woman's survival was at risk. If the family were to break up, the man could take his brawn and farming skills and start a new family. The woman, having invested her human capital in children specific to that marriage, would have less rather than more value on the marriage market after making her investment. Although she could take her children into another marriage, there is evidence that males have a strong, "hard-wired" preference for their own offspring.[17] While the male's human capital increases with the experience of farming, the external value of the female's human capital declines with every child.

We can see here how the issue of credible commitment enters the bargaining story. Without a credible male commitment to marriage women could be made worse off in the case of divorce than without entering marriage and having children in the first place. Since opportunities for women outside marriage were few, and with no insurance against violence and old age, the extent of the male commitment was correspondingly limited.

Legal provisions made divorce difficult, and alimony made it costly, but this did not prevent many men from effectively establishing independent lives outside the household, leaving their wives and children to live on a bare minimum. Yet we can discern here the origins of a phenomenon that at first blush can appear paradoxical: women are often the most vigorous defenders of social norms and legal codes that people often (rightly) view as manifestations of female subordination.[18] As we will see in a later chapter, the modern gender gap, in which women hold less traditionalist views on the family and politics, is a thoroughly modern phenomenon that is still limited to a relatively small number of postindustrial societies.

The bargaining power of males in agrarian societies translates into norms as parents socialize their children to make the best use of opportunities available to them. In an economy where male brawn commands a premium, a family would risk genetic obliteration in one generation if it reared daughters to resist male authority and to enjoy their sexuality on their own terms. Because in an agrarian society a woman's peak value is realized when she is young, fertile, and unencumbered with another man's progeny, parents would want to instill in daughters the importance of preparing for the marriage market, for that is their single chance to secure their livelihood. Where economic efficiency gives males a bargaining advantage on account of greater mobility of their human capital from a gendered division of labor, families do best by socializing a daughter to cultivate the femininity that will help her win her a good man and the docility that will help her keep him. Because human history has been agrarian for most of recorded time, these are the values—let's call it patriarchy—most familiar to humanity.

Industrialization

Mechanization and the widespread introduction of labor-saving devices have ushered in a new era of complex and interdependent markets; but for our purposes, the most important *long-term* effect of industrialization has been to increase female bargaining power by reducing the premium to brawn. Early industrialization, however, may actually *reduce* rather than increase female labor force participation, if we include piece work by farmers' wives as market labor, and given that in early stages of industrialization the available work is often loud, dirty, and dangerous— perhaps still claiming a premium on male brawn.[19] The emergence of more varied kinds of market work eventually draws women into the labor market, particularly with the rise of service jobs in retail, banking, insurance, and clerical work that accompany later phases of industrialization. In time, the opportunity costs of keeping women at home overwhelm the inertial attachment to a gendered specialization of labor.

We take the growing acceptance of gender equality in industrialized societies to reflect the diminution of the male brawn premium that existed for millennia of agrarian history. By the late nineteenth and early twentieth centuries, women in developed countries were no longer owned, literally, by their fathers and husbands, and they were given the right to vote. As women moved increasingly into labor markets, the idea that both parents are responsible for child rearing has gained acceptance, and views that women are less capable than men have become taboo. Men finally found it in their interests to allow women to work in order to supplement the family income as remunerative opportunities for female labor increased.[20] In addition, female bargaining power within families has grown as their exit options to marriage have improved. In response to this different opportunity structure for females, parents have adapted by providing their daughters with more educational preparation and by teaching girls how to survive in a competitive labor market—not just to snare a husband for life.

A male premium lingers, however, in industrial societies. Not only do some manufacturing processes utilize human strength; more important, many manufacturing processes can make use of increasing returns to human capital where, the longer one does the job, the better one gets at it. Firms may want to exploit this phenomenon by committing to long-term employment contracts and investing in the employee's on-the-job training and skills acquisition. This can hurt the employment chances of women, given their higher probability of quitting or reducing their hours to bear and rear children. Elsewhere we have argued that economies with strong specific skills production processes will discourage women from the labor market by increasing the costs to the employer and employee of career interruption on account of family work.[21] Subtle differences in social norms might follow from these differences in opportunities across the sexes. Japanese girls, for example, are still taught to speak in a feminine and deferential way—two characteristics that remain virtually synonymous in Japan. This is not surprising given the expectation of lifetime employment in Japan's labor markets and therefore the strong preference for employees who will not burden the company with time off for childbirth and rearing.

Postindustrial Service Economies

Women's work opportunities expand even further in postindustrial service economies with the availability of general skills jobs that are not characterized by increasing returns to specific human capital and that therefore do not penalize women for career interruption on account of childbearing and rearing. Postindustrial employment includes for us both jobs in the service sector, such as retail, finance, insurance, health care, as well as clerical work in the manufacturing industry. What sets postindustrialization apart from service employment expansion under industrialization is that service sector employment—especially in social and personal services—grows at the same time as industrial employment declines, a pattern we document below. During industrialization, female clerical work in the manufacturing sector may be suppressed in countries with strong labor protections because companies need to deploy otherwise redundant males to whose employment they are committed. Much of Japan's clerical work, for example, is done by men in "lifetime employment" careers.[22] But the move toward a postindustrial economy creates an irresistible force of change: when employing women became as efficient as hiring men—or more to the point, when not employing capable women became inefficient—women began to move into the workforce in large numbers.

The connection between service sector employment and female labor force participation is a strikingly close one. Figure 2.2 shows that female labor force participation in OECD countries closely tracks the rise in service employment. During the 1950s and 1960s most of this employment was linked to a female life-cycle pattern where women left the labor market when they married and started families and reentered as the children reached adulthood. Women never became financially independent from men, and they had strong incentives to favor policies that maximized the income of the male breadwinner and strengthened the family as an institution. This continues to be the case for many women, but starting in the 1970s the rising opportunities for paid employment gave some women an option of real financial independence, which in turn led to a rise in divorce rates as many women left bad marriages. It is this combination of rising di-

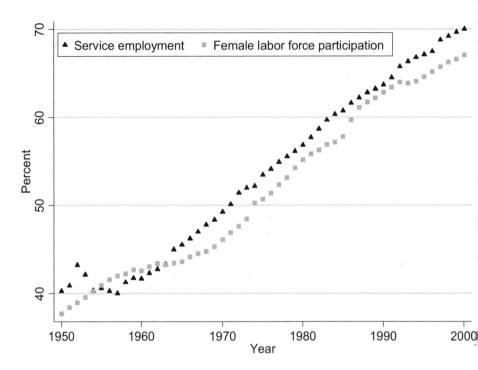

Figure 2.2. Service employment and female labor force participation, 1950–2000 (OECD)
Source: OECD, *Labour Force Statistics* (Paris: OECD, various years).

vorce rates and prospects of financial independence, we argue, that is the origin of new gender norms and socialization patterns. No doubt, the end of the postwar boom by the early 1970s also drew into the labor force many women for whom the insufficiency of a single male breadwinner income was a greater impetus than independence. But regardless of their motives, women marched into the workforce on a large scale only where and when there was a sizable demand for female labor.

We have explained the link between service employment and female labor force participation in terms of two factors: a smaller brawn premium in the services industry, and the high general skills content of jobs in much of the services industry, which reduces the costs to employers of career interruption associated with specific skills manufacturing.

The clearest evidence for the latter thesis comes from data on the gender composition of particular occupations, based on the Standard Classification of Occupations (ISCO-88) by the International Labor Organization (ILO). Ignoring military personnel, ISCO-88 contains nine broad occupational groups, which are subdivided into numerous subgroups depending on the specialization of skills represented within each major group. The number of subgroups varies according to the size of the labor market covered by that major group and the degree of skill specialization within each group. By dividing the share of subgroups in a particular major group by the share of the labor force in those groups we can get a rough measure of the degree of specificity of skills represented by each major group.[23] In figure 2.3 we have related this measure to the percent share of women in the different occupations for the most recent year available (2000). The numbers are averages for the thirteen countries for which we have comparable ISCO-88 data. Bolded occupations are those that have disproportionately large numbers of low-skilled and low-paid jobs.

Note the strong negative relationship with men dominating occupations that require highly specialized skills—a pattern that is repeated in every one of our thirteen cases. Not surprisingly, these jobs are in agriculture and manufacturing rather than in services.

Conversely, although men on average participate more in the labor market than women, women are relatively overrepresented in service sector jobs that require general skills—a clear sign of comparative advantage (even as many of these jobs are low skill as indicated in boldface).[24] The link to the previous figure is straightforward: the occupations in which women are well represented are the ones that have expanded most rapidly over the past thirty to forty years, propelling women into the labor market and unambiguously improving their economic independence from men, as argued by Goldin and others (Goldin 1990).

As with the other economic systems we have reviewed, postindustrial societies tend to have a set of gender norms that reinforce the most efficient strategies for securing a stable livelihood for children of both sexes. With the possibility of independent livelihood outside of marriage, the bargaining position of women has improved, leading to a steady assault on patriarchal norms. Parents in developed economies no longer fear that assertive daughters will be consigned to lifelong poverty and misery on ac-

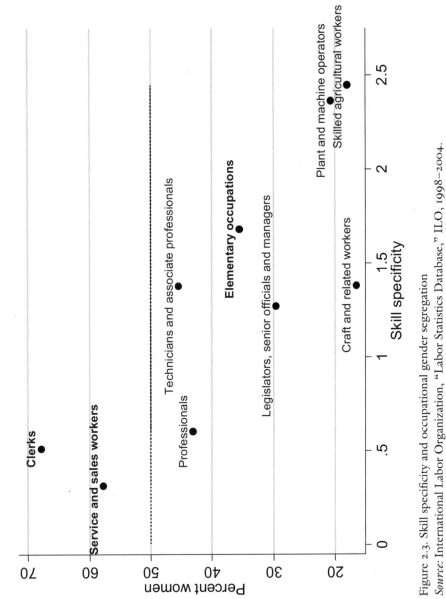

Figure 2.3. Skill specificity and occupational gender segregation

Source: International Labor Organization, "Labor Statistics Database," ILO, 1998–2004.

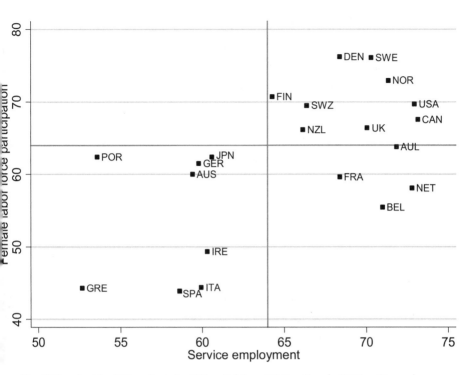

Key: AUS = Austria; AUL = Australia; BEL = Belgium; CAN = Canada; DEN = Denmark;
FIN = Finland; FRA = France; GER = Germany; GRE = Greece; IRE = Ireland; ITA = Italy;
JPN = Japan; NET = Netherlands; NOR = Norway; NZL = New Zealand; POR = Portugal;
SWE = Sweden; SWZ = Switzerland; UK = United Kingdom; USA = United States.

Figure 2.4. Service employment and female labor force participation (1990s)
Source: OECD, *Labour Force Statistics* (Paris: OECD, various years).

count of losing out on marriage, itself no longer a prerequisite to their
survival. We expect instead for them to teach their daughters to optimize
across the marriage and work markets to ensure their long-term welfare
and happiness and for the marriage market to be a smaller part of the welfare equation in the minds of most parents.

This is not to deny that the opportunities for paid female employment
are still shaped by domestic economic and political conditions. This point
is illustrated in figure 2.4, which shows the cross-national relationship be-

tween service employment and female labor force participation in the 1990s. According to the data, both service employment and female labor force participation were high in the Nordic countries and the liberal market economies. The latter rely heavily on general skills and flexible labor markets, which offer good opportunities for female employment, although there is a strong division among women along class lines. Indeed, the availability of low-paid services is one of the conditions for the expansion of market-based services. This is not true in Scandinavia, where there is more reliance on industry- and occupational-specific skills and highly compressed wages. In these countries female employment is enabled by a large feminized public service sector (about 80 percent are women), which combines relatively secure employment with flexibility that allows women to balance work and family. Public sector employment is clearly politically constructed, a fact to which we will return. The main point we wish to make here is that the jump in female employment between manufacturing and services may be as large as that between agriculture and manufacturing, with profound implications for social values about the proper roles of men and women in the economy.

Gender Norms and Human Mate Selection

This section introduces empirical data to test the proposition that norms, over long periods of time, reflect the bargaining relationship between the genders that economic structure and organization imply. Ideally, long-run panel data on gender stereotypes would allow us to evaluate how production structures shape attitudes toward women and their "proper roles" across countries and within countries over the longue durée. No such data exist. Instead, we make use of David Buss's study of human mate preferences in thirty-seven cultures (Buss 1989) to see how labor market opportunities for women affect gender stereotypes with respect to the ideal mate.[25] Buss, an evolutionary psychologist, used his data to make the point that human mate preferences are hardwired and are therefore remarkably uniform across cultures. Although this is undoubtedly true for many aspects of mate preferences—including good looks, emotional stability, good health, favorable social status, and even good financial prospects—some of Buss's variables refer to social aspects of gender relations that our argument is designed to explain. While we agree that norms are not a reflection of culture, we expect socially malleable norms about desirable mate attributes to change as the economic independence of women increases.

There are three variables in the Buss data that are candidates for such an interpretation: the importance attached to chastity, being a good cook and housekeeper, and having a desire for home and children (referred to as simply "desire for family" in figure 2.5). In male-dominated societies, especially agricultural ones, chastity is a norm that restricts the use of the only mobile "asset" of women: their sexuality. An inviolable norm of chastity restricts sex to an activity that can occur only inside the marriage and thereby also restricts the ability of women to use sex for bargaining purposes. Of course, the limits of norms are constantly tested and sometimes broken—much of world literature would not exist otherwise!—but societies where men hold most of the power can be expected to develop norms of chastity as an expression of such power. Yet in postindustrial societies where women have high mobility out of a marriage, chastity is an unsustainable, and inefficient, norm. If men insisted on virginity in this context, they would severely limit the pool of potential mates. Hence the movement from agricultural to postindustrial economies should be associated with a decline in the importance placed on chastity.

If we are right that females were economically viable without a male patron in hunter-gatherer societies, and if this is the "environment" of early evolutionary adaptation, there is no reason for men and women to be genetically coded to have mate preferences that reflect a particular sexual division of labor. It makes good sense for men to seek women who are good cooks and housekeepers, or have a strong desire for home and children, in societies where the structure of the economy induces a strict "traditional" gender division of labor but not in societies where women have economic opportunities outside the family that rival those of men. In these cases, men who consider only women with traditional homemaker skills will severely limit the available market for desirable mates.

The malleability of sexual norms, and certain mate preferences, is in fact reflected in the Buss data. For example, when respondents are asked about the importance of female chastity on a scale ranging from 3 (indispensable) to 0 (irrelevant or unimportant), the average for former Yugoslavia is 0.08, and the average for China is 2.61 (referring to the mid-1980s). The variation in the variables "good cook and housekeeper" and "desire for home and children" is somewhat lower but still considerable: between 1.1 and 2.1 for the former and 0.9 and 2.8 for the latter (again, the feasible range is from 0 to 3). Buss's emphasis on constancy notwithstanding, variation of this magnitude invites explanations such as ours that relate variability in gender stereotypes, including mate preferences, to the relative economic opportunities available to men and women.

The Buss data were collected from thirty-seven "cultures," which generally coincide with the boundaries of nation-states and represent a range of geographic regions, ethnicities, and levels of development. The data set consists of 10,047 individual-level observations, which are averaged for each of the thirty-seven cultures. We focus on thirty-one of these cases because they refer to countries (not ethnicities) for which we have comparative data on potential independent variables. In the case of the United States, Buss, Shackleford, Kirkpatrick, and Larsen (2001) build a data set from existing surveys dating back to 1939, and we make some use of these longitudinal data to examine cross-time trends. The individual-level data are unfortunately of little use for our purposes because they contain virtually no relevant political economy variables.[26]

Buss and coauthors emphasize the relative cultural universality of mate preferences (including male preference for chastity and beauty and female preference for males with more resources), but we note the very significant changes in the three variables in the U.S. case. Buss, Shackleford, Kirkpatrick, and Larsen speculate briefly about the causes of these changes (the pill in the case of chastity and increased use of domestic help in the case of the good cook and housekeeper variable), but we see the changes to be closely related to broader structural-economic differences across time and space. Mate preferences should be quite different in agricultural societies compared to industrial and especially service-intensive economies because of differences in the economic position of women. Where women face good labor market prospects, they are less reliant on finding a spouse who can support them, and attributes such as chastity or desire to care for the family ought to decline in importance as male mate selection criteria.

In fact, empirical evidence bears this out: mate preferences seem to change with the structure of the economy. In our simple cross-national OLS (Ordinary Least Squares) analysis, presented in appendix B table 2.2

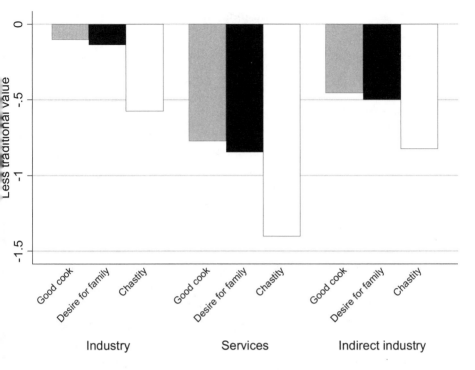

Figure 2.5. The effect of sector on support for traditional values (negative numbers indicate less traditional values compared to the most agricultural economy)
Note: Each bar shows the predicted effect of changing sectoral employment from the lowest to the highest values observed in the Buss sample of countries based on the regression results in appendix B. The first two groups show the estimated *direct* effects of industry and services. The last group shows the estimated *indirect* effects of industrial employment, which are calculated by multiplying the coefficient on industry when service employment is regressed on industry employment (.86) with the coefficients on the direct effects of services.
Source: Buss 1989.

and illustrated in figure 2.5, the exogenous sector variables are the shares of total employment in industry and services (the dependent variable, again, varies between 0 and 3).[27] Since those not employed in these sectors are engaged in agriculture, agriculture serves as the reference group. In a simple regression with industrial and service employment as explanatory variables, both reduce the emphasis adults place on traditional values. But the direct effect is much stronger—and statistically significant—for services. Although this seems to suggest that it is the service economy, not the industrial economy, that transforms norms, one has to be cautious with such an interpretation because industrial employment and service employment are compositional variables that rise in tandem through long periods of economic history (at the expense of agriculture). Indeed, the initial rise of services came *as a result of* the industrial revolution, and it was not until the 1960s that the expansion of services started to be associated with a decline in industry in some countries. In figure 2.5 this is shown by the notable indirect effect of industrial employment. But the weak direct effect of industrial employment *does* tell us that the rise of manufacturing jobs has not always been a boon to female employment because these jobs tended to emphasize brawn or specific skills, with the exception of some low-skill occupations (elementary occupations in figure 2.3). Service employment is the mechanism through which industrialization had an effect, and it becomes an exogenous engine of change during the period of postindustrialization from some time in the 1960s (in most OECD countries).

The results do not change dramatically when controlling for Western culture and fertility rates (shown in table 2.2 in appendix B). One might suppose that the decline in traditional gender norms reflects the rise of a secular and decadent Western culture, occasioned not by any economic laws of change but by excessive individualism, an explosion of popular culture, and lack of moral leadership. Yet it is only in the case of chastity that the Western dummy seems to add explanatory power, and even here it does not eliminate the importance of economic sector. Fertility rates seem to matter even less, although it is common to suppose that the pill, and the accompanying decline in fertility, has caused a transformation in gender norms. In the case of chastity, the effect of the fertility variable is actually in the wrong direction.

While the importance of the employment structure stands up to controls, it is true that the composition of employment is almost perfectly collinear with economic development, which makes it impossible for regressions to control for development. A broader process of economic development could be driving the story in some sense, and certainly economic development is correlated with female labor market opportunities. Yet we think it is instructive to distinguish the effects of industry and services on norms because they matter in quite different ways as we have shown. For more than a century, industrialization was the engine of economic development in Europe, but the transformation of gender norms was glacial compared

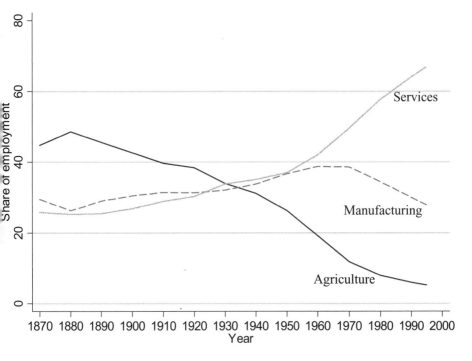

Figure 2.6. The sectoral composition of employment in seventeen OECD countries, 1870–1995
Note: The observations are averages for seventeen OECD countries by decade.

to the effect of postindustrialization in the past four decades. The reason norms changed with industrialization can be attributed almost entirely to the accompanying rise in services. Considering that many manual jobs in manufacturing were as unappealing to women as agricultural labor, this is unsurprising, and it shows why it is not sufficient to simply focus on economic development. It is not wealth but opportunities in the labor market that matter.

Because industrialization did not merely replace agricultural labor with tough manual jobs in the manufacturing sector—but also vastly expanded the number of secretaries, retailers, maids, accountants, insurance agents, merchants, and bankers—it had a transforming effect on gender norms. This is illustrated by the long-term employment trends depicted in figure 2.6.

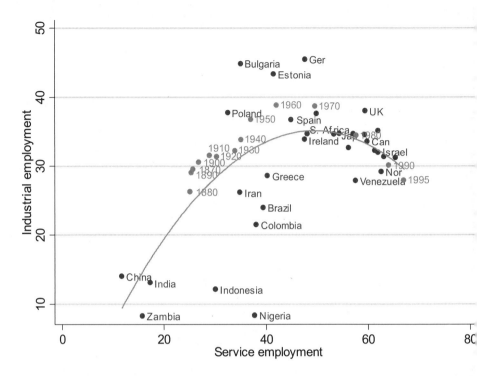

Figure 2.7. Relationship between service and industrial employment
Note: The country observations are for the countries in the Buss data (some names omitted); the decade observations are averages for seventeen OECD countries. The solid line is the predicted relationship when regressing industrial employment on service employment and its square.

Starting around the beginning of the industrial revolution in 1870, the graph shows how the rise of industrial and service employment went hand in hand, at the expense of agricultural employment, until the 1960s (for a sample of seventeen OECD countries). From then on industrial employment begins to decline (along with agriculture), while service employment expands at an even faster rate.

Figure 2.7 illustrates this curvilinear relationship using both the intertemporal data on employment from figure 2.6 (by decade) and the cross-sectional figures for the countries in the Buss data (by country name). Note from the intertemporal data how employment in industry and services rise in tandem until industry accounts for about 40 percent employment. At that point services start to grow at the expense of industry. Given that a very similar pattern holds for the cross-sectional data, it is sensible to treat countries in the Buss data as if they are on different developmental stages. With that assumption in mind we can then use the cross-sectional regression results to simulate mate preferences through time. In addition, because some data on mate preferences are available over time in the U.S. case, we are also able to check whether the historical simulations match the actual data in this country.

Figure 2.8 shows the results of this simulation. If the key assumption holds (that is, countries in the Buss data are on different developmental stages), it is clear that manufacturing employment as such has not been particularly conducive to the economic empowerment of women, or to gender equality, but the expansion of services that accompanies industrialization has. Roughly half (49 percent) of the total estimated change in mate preferences since 1870 occurs during the ninety years of industrialization from 1870 to 1960. The rest occurs during the thirty-five years of deindustrialization from 1960 to 1995. Industrialization clearly helped transform gender norms, but deindustrialization greatly accelerated this transformation.[28] Changes in the sectoral structure of the economy, especially the rise of general skills services, go a long way toward explaining, or at least predicting, changes in mate preferences.

Again, our simulations assume that the cross-sectional regression results are applicable across time, and we do not have any long-term survey data similar to those in figure 2.7 to test this assumption. We do, however, have mate preference data for nearly half a century (1939–1996) for the United States. The evolution of preferences across the three variables in this case is shown by dotted lines in figure 2.8. They generally follow the simulated trend, and one should not make too much of deviations for individual years since the samples are small, unrepresentative, and not consistently polled over time. In 1956, for example, the numbers are based on just 120 undergraduate students at University of Wisconsin at Madison. Other samples have different sizes and are from different universities. Giving these limitations, it is actually quite remarkable that the changes in the United States are so similar to the simulated changes based on the cross-sectional

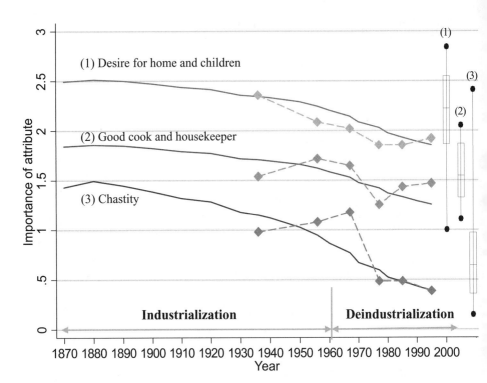

Figure 2.8. Simulated mate preferences in seventeen countries, 1870–1995
Note: The solid lines are the predicted preferences for particular attributes in potential mates based on the regression results in table 2.2 and historical data on the average sectoral composition of employment. The connected diamonds are the averages for the United States based on actual historical data on the rankings of preferred attributes. The scale on the y-axis uses the entire range of the preference variable. The "box and whisker" plots on the right show the median, the range, and the interquartile difference for each variable.

data.[29] It gives us confidence that economic structure, or mode of production more generally, is historically linked to changing attitudes about desirable attributes in a marriage partner. Because the effect is most intimately related to service employment, where women are at the least disadvantage in the labor market, the causal mechanism that we have posited also seems to be operating.

In particular, we have suggested that the availability of remunerative employment for women changes the dynamics of gender socialization. Instead of rearing daughters solely for the marriage market, families begin to think of their children's economic chances more equally. The social glorification of virginity declines as it loses its economic grip. Being a good cook and a good parent, while perhaps always desirable attributes in a mate, become less salient and no longer the sole province of the female partner. In chapter 5 we extend this analysis to explain individual norms and policy preferences.

Conclusions

Patriarchal values, we have suggested, may be thought of as an internalized reckoning of relative bargaining power. When the alternatives to marriage are systematically weaker for females than for their male partners, it does not require a brutish man to keep his wife in submission. If her parents and social community have done their job, she will have learned as a girl the importance of virginity until marriage (though she may not think of it as a strategy for marrying "up"), and she will have cultivated many qualities to keep her husband pleased with her (though she may not consider these qualities as a means to maintain her livelihood). For her, as perhaps for her forebears, these are not schemes but are normal, commonsensical, perhaps even morally mandated ways to live. Patriarchy, when other options are unworkable, does not require a big stick, and even great philosophers like Rousseau are fooled into believing that it is the natural order of things.

The ability to walk away from the status quo confers bargaining power that is not available to women in agricultural economies where the premium to male brawn makes inefficient, perhaps even unviable, female employment on a par with a man's. We have argued that industrialization and, even more dramatically, the rise of the service sector are transforming social values by providing women with alternatives to unsatisfying marriages. Once employment opportunities for women have approached those of men in quantity and quality, socialization begins to shift away from "playing the marriage market." The declining importance of virginity, along with lower male expectations of homemaking skills in a spouse, reflects a change in the way parents prepare their children for life and liveli-hood.

As this value change gains momentum it accelerates other changes in so-ciety because women who do not accept subservient marital roles will be more concerned about their bargaining power within the marriage, seek independent careers, and advise their daughters to do the same. As we will see in chapter 5, this is likely to be accompanied by gendered political pref-erences where women favor government policies that facilitate their abil-ity to balance family and careers, further undermining a stark gendered division of labor.

Appendix A: A Brief Primer on Bargaining within the Household

Figure 2.9 shows a very simple bargaining game between a male and a female within a household, where the household itself is viewed as a contract ("marriage"). The total product of the household, broadly con-ceived to include all material and nonmaterial benefits, is normalized to one and assumed to be divisible. The thick contract line is the feasible set of bargained outcomes, assuming that the household contract produces a net surplus compared to a situation without a contract. The bargaining set is bounded by the spouses' "outside options" (O_M and O_F), which are the payoffs each partner can get if he or she leaves the household (leading to a "divorce"). The outside options, in turn, can be conceptualized as the returns on mobile or general or marketable assets (G_M and G_F) *minus* foregone returns on any household-specific assets (S_M and S_F), which are not marketable. Assuming away any first mover advantage, as well as any systematic differences in the patience of household members or their level of risk aversion, the Rubinstein bargaining solution is simply the midpoint on the contract curve. This point is called R1 in the figure.

As long as R1 is within the outside options, the latter are irrelevant (this is called the bargaining space in the graph). By the same token a shift in the outside options will not have any effect on the outcome as long as the bargained outcome is still inside the bargaining space. The irrelevance of outside options is called the outside option principle (OOPS) in bargain-ing theory (Osborne and Rubinstein 1994, 128). The reason is that any

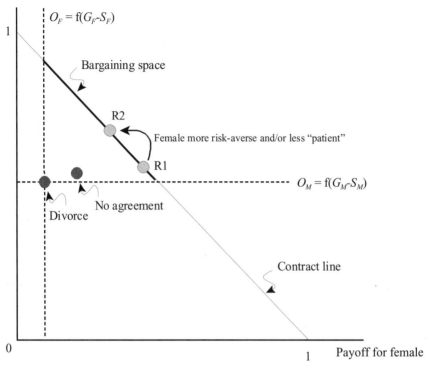

Figure 2.9. A simple household bargaining game

threat to leave the household for the outside option is not credible as long as it is better for both to stay in the household. Noncredible threats should be ignored. Outside options may of course exceed what the marriage provides for either party, and then they are credible. During long periods of human history men have enjoyed so much better outside options on account of their movable assets that these options may have been binding on the marriage contract.

But they probably did even better than that. The reason is that outside options cannot easily be separated from "inside options." Inside options determine the division of the marital surplus within the family, subject to the outside constraints (that is, a particular point in the bargaining space).

They are determined by the relative patience of the two parties in achieving an agreement—or alternatively by their relative tolerance of living with no agreement (one of the dark-shaded points in figure 2.9)—and by their relative aversion to the risk that the marriage ends in a divorce after a protracted negotiation over who gets what. It stands to reason that the party to a negotiation who has more to lose if the contract breaks down is more risk-averse. At R1 in figure 2.9, this is clearly the woman (note the distance between R1 and the divorce breakdown point). Yet since R1 is very close to the male's outside option, he can afford to be less concerned than the woman that an aggressive bargaining stance may lead to a dissolution of the marriage. Such a difference in risk-aversion shifts the bargained outcome toward the male's ideal point (say R2). The same is true for patience. If there is no agreement, the male will have access to most or all of the family's cash flow. This does not have to be shared, yet the woman will find it harder to withhold the benefits of household labor. The man is therefore in a position to hold out longer for a better deal (that is, be more patient). This again favors the male and shifts the outcome toward his ideal point.

In general, although a large number of individual factors affect inside options, the ability to work away from a deal without losing too much is a major advantage, and this ability is closely related to the investments that have been made in marketable as opposed to household-specific assets. Bargaining power can therefore be roughly approximated as a function of the ratio of outside options of the spouses, which are themselves determined by the difference between mobile and household-specific assets.

An important complication to the analysis needs to be noted: the efficiency gains from marriage presuppose specialization, yet such specialization undermines the outside options of women. In the Becker model, the woman specializes completely in household-specific skills and enters the labor market (typically on a part-time basis) only when the time available for work exceeds the amount of required household labor (primarily before children are born and after they leave the household). Conversely, the male specializes exclusively in marketable skills. In the Becker model this stark division of labor is not problematic for the woman because of two key assumptions: (1) all market earnings will be shared for the collective benefit of the family, and (2) the marriage contract itself cannot be revoked. If the first assumption is violated, the only way that the woman can strengthen her ability to affect the allocation of household income is by gaining access to her own stream of income, which requires entry into paid work. If the second assumption is violated, neither spouse can ignore his or her welfare in the event of divorce, which in turn depends on outside options and again undermines the incentive to invest in household-specific skills. The problem then is that without a credible long-term commitment to sharing and to the marriage itself, the full efficiency gains from specialization will not be realized.

Credible commitment problems have to be solved through institutions when reputation alone is not sufficient. In particular, when the potential efficiency gains from marriage are large—which we have argued is especially true in agricultural societies—we would expect strong community and legal norms to balance the bargaining advantage of the male by establishing a set of family responsibilities for the head of the household and recognizing marriage as a "sacred" institution that can be dissolved only under exceptional circumstances. Patriarchy thus goes with strong protections of marriage as an institution, as well as with norms against abandonment by the head of the household.

Appendix B: Cross-National Regression Analysis of Mate Preferences

Table 2.2. Mate preferences as a function of economic sector

	Good cook and housekeeper		Desire for home and children		Chastity	
Industrial employment	−0.003 (0.005)	0.002 (0.008)	−0.004 (0.009)	0.013 (0.013)	−0.018 (0.010)	−0.001 (0.013)
Service employment	−0.014** (0.004)	−0.014** (0.004)	−0.016* (0.006)	−0.011* (0.007)	−0.027** (0.007)	−0.017* (0.007)
Western culture	—	0.084 (0.170)	—	−0.348 (0.278)	—	−0.923* (0.280)
Fertility rate	—	0.085 (0.054)	—	0.100 (0.089)	—	−0.069 (0.089)
Constant	2.293** (0.160)	1.858 (0.332)	3.006** (0.259)	2.325** (0.544)	2.823** (0.289)	2.584** (0.547)
Adj. R-squared	.451	.481	.262	.297	.576	.651
N	31	31	31	31	31	31

Sources: Buss 1989; OECD, *Labour Force Statistics* (Paris: OECD, various years).
Key: *Significant at .05 level; **significant at .01 level (two-tailed test)

3

THE GENDER DIVISION OF LABOR, OR
WHY WOMEN WORK DOUBLE SHIFTS

On average, women participate less in the labor market than men, whereas they assume the lion's share of unpaid work in the household. Economists have traditionally explained this pattern as the outcome of a coordination game where a more or less complete division of labor is the efficient solution due to increasing returns to human capital: people get better and better at the tasks they undertake, so a division of labor makes sense.[1] Although the biological advantages of women specializing in household skills are slim in a modern economy, their gravitating toward household work may be reinforced by childhood socialization in which parents seek to maximize the success of their children later in life. Since gender roles are assigned before "true" preferences are observable, the coordination game is solved by using inherently small gender differences as the cue.

But although the efficiency model captures some key aspects of the family as an institution, levels of female labor force participation are actually quite varied across countries at comparable levels of development. The efficiency model also fails to explain why there is so much variance in the distribution of housework between the sexes *after* controlling for hours spent in paid work and earnings. Depending on the country, hours worked in the marketplace have a big effect—or not—on how evenly household work is shared between the sexes.

The *division of labor puzzle* can only be understood by treating marriage as an incomplete contract that is potentially subject to termination.[2]

When both members of the couple recognize that the marriage could fail, each has an incentive to cultivate their outside options by entering into paid work. The distribution of unpaid work is then determined by bargaining, where bargaining power is dependent on political-economic factors outside the family. We make use of recent political economy arguments[3] as a well as macrosociological work on the welfare state[4] to tie broad economic conditions to intrafamily bargaining over the division of labor.

The rest of the chapter lays out the standard efficiency model of the family division of labor as well as the bargaining model alternative that better fits today's world. Empirically we find that, controlling for a variety of factors, women with stronger outside employment options are able to reduce their share of family work. These options in turn reflect not only individual attributes like age and education but also differences in economic institutions, family policy, and the role of the public sector.

Explaining the Gender Division of Labor

In the economic efficiency model of the family, couples engage in a division of labor to take advantage of gains from trade.[5] One family member will specialize in marketable skills and paid work, and another will specialize in household skills and unpaid work, on grounds that there are increasing returns to human capital in both domains, and that the care of children cannot be completely subcontracted out without loss to the children's well-being. The spouse specializing in household skills may enter the labor market part time if the domestic workload permits this—something that is more likely to be the case early and late in a marriage corresponding to the years before children are born and after they start school or leave the household.

Since dividing the work is in principle a pure coordination game, either the husband or the wife could specialize in market or household skills, but women will almost invariably specialize in the latter because of an initial comparative biological advantage in caring for very young children. This advantage, however, may last only for the first months of a child's life, and it is not hard to imagine distributions of preferences for type of work across the sexes that would lead to a far more even average division of family responsibilities and paid work than we actually observe.

The economist Gary Becker, who formalized the efficiency model, solved this puzzle in two ways. First, a small comparative advantage is magnified by increasing returns to human capital—people get better at tasks as they accumulate experience.[6] Second, parents have an incentive to prepare their children for responsibilities they will assume later in life, and this may reinforce the gender division of labor by instilling preferences through childhood socialization. Since children are unlikely to reveal their true role dispositions at a very early age, parents choose to socialize their children in skills that they are most likely to be good at, or even more reflexively, that society assigns. If females grow up thinking it is normal for them to stay at home with the kids, this magnifies biological differences and solves the family coordination problem later in life.

In hindsight (Becker developed his argument in the early 1960s) it is easy to ridicule Becker's model as an intellectual justification for the traditional male-dominated 1950s family. But it is precisely the capacity of the model to account for the stark gender division of labor and the differences in the socialization of girls and boys in the traditional family that makes it so powerful. Still, it is clear that something fundamental has changed in a number of countries in North America and Europe. The division of labor by sex is less pronounced and socialization less gendered than a few decades ago. Families in the United States, for example, are more likely to teach their girls to be assertive and independent than was the case some decades ago or than is still true in countries where female labor market opportunities are more restricted.[7]

One factor that looms large in the explanation of these changes is the rise in divorce rates. Whether divorce rates are a response to exogenous changes in divorce law or whether divorce is endogenous to a growth in labor market opportunities for women, divorce is now an accepted part of modern life in most rich democracies. In 1950 the probability that a first marriage would end in divorce was one in five in the United States, and any behavior that could conceivably lead to divorce—infidelity but also overt challenges to established gender roles—was considered taboo by widely held religious and community norms. Today the divorce rate is one in two for first marriages and is now considered an acceptable, even desirable, solution to marital problems.

The ease of divorce makes a tremendous difference to the Becker framework because spouses must now concern themselves with what they can do to secure their welfare in the event that the marriage breaks up. In other words, their outside options become crucial. And if we want to understand the implications of this for the division of labor and patterns of socialization, we have to treat family members as individuals with distinct preferences. The shorthand of treating the family as a unitary actor is less useful than it may once have been.

The most obvious potential conflict of interest concerns the division of labor—precisely the variable Becker's model was designed to explain. The problem is that heavy investment in household-specific skills is likely to undermine outside options. Not only will such investments crowd out investments in marketable skills, but the value of marketable skills is likely to be seriously reduced by longer absences from the labor market.[8]

In principle, household skills can be "sold" on the remarriage market, but since one critical "skill" in this market is to produce and nurture offspring, a woman's position in the remarriage market will be seriously reduced as soon as she has children in another marriage. Adding insult to injury, another valuable commodity in the remarriage market is youth and beauty, which also deteriorates with time. Hence, even in the remarriage market, the only nonperishable commodity is earnings power—and perhaps also the attractiveness that comes with education and an active lifestyle.

From one perspective, investing in household-specific skills presents a long-term commitment problem. As we suggested in the previous chapter, when the gains from specialization are very large we would expect that legal and social norms (perhaps also religious ones) would make the marriage contract very difficult to terminate. But when the gains are smaller, it becomes harder to justify anything that approximates prohibition, and as access to divorce improves, the incentives to invest in household-specific skills decline, creating a snowball effect. Divorce rates are thus at least partly endogenous to the gains from specialization—a theme we will return to in chapter 5 when we consider family policy preferences—but this does not change the fact that in a high-divorce equilibrium the division of labor will be contested. This is true even for segments of the population that may benefit from a complete division of labor since it is impossible to have different rules for divorce for different groups. In this sense, divorce rates are an exogenous variable.

In the context of high divorce, since labor market participation is essential to cultivate outside options, women have strong reasons to resist a complete division of labor in the family. But by the same token men have an incentive to resist taking on more domestic responsibilities. Bargaining models of marriage capture this by assuming that compromises have to be found in a bargaining space that is constrained by the outside options. The simplest conception of outside options is whatever utility either party can get outside the marriage. But some models also allow for the possibility of noncooperative outcomes without divorce where spouses recede into separate "spheres" characterized by more or less separate finances, partially divided living spaces, and general mutual avoidance.[9]

In either formulation, opportunities in the labor market shape outside options and hence the marriage bargaining space. As we explained in the previous chapter, in a Rubinstein bargaining model the solution to the game must be found inside the constraints of the outside options, and the latter also tends to increase the risk each player is willing to take that a tough bargaining stance, with a potentially high payoff, could end in divorce. Willingness to take risks in turn improves a player's bargaining power and shifts the outcome of the game toward the spouse with the better outside option. So if outside options are equally attractive to both sides, we would predict an even distribution of household work. More realistically, since women's outside options tend to be inferior to men's, women will tend to do more of the household work. But women have a strong incentive to resist the complete division of labor that would be optimal in the Becker model.[10] This incentive rises with the probability that a marriage will end in divorce since the expected cumulative returns on household-specific investments will be smaller and since the insurance motive (making sure you are OK in the event of divorce) will figure more prominently in the calculation. The division of labor is therefore in part a function of the divorce probability, which plays no role in efficiency models.[11]

Since household bargaining may lead to a less complete, and hence less efficient, division of labor, it is logically conceivable that an explicit marriage contract could compensate women for the risks of specialization in household skills and the associated deterioration of marketable skills. This could be done by guaranteeing a lump sum severance payment or the sharing of future income streams, such as alimony and child support, in the event of divorce. But to prevent problems of moral hazard, shirking, and other well-known maladies of incomplete information, such prenuptial agreements would have to stipulate all relevant contingencies in advance —including just cause for divorce, fair treatment of the other party in the marriage, the division of custody in the event of divorce, and penalties for noncompliance with any stipulations in the contract. Precisely this type of detailed marriage contracting has reached almost farcical complexity among Hollywood celebrities where the stakes and divorce rates are both very high. But few would claim that prenuptial agreements constitute a general solution to incomplete marriage contracting, and they are in fact rare. Just as in nonstandard economic contracting, comprehensive ex ante agreements are either impractical or prohibitively expensive to write and enforce.

In this chapter we focus on the bargaining process between two spouses and leave the degree of efficiency loss from the breakdown in specialization as an open empirical question. If, for example, child care could be subcontracted without loss of child welfare, we might expect couples to abandon much of the specialization of labor without efficiency loss.[12] This reduces the need to bargain over household labor. But the cost of child care is of course very much a matter of public policy, and preferences over these policies, which we examine in chapter 5, can be understood within the bargaining framework we use. Besides, time budget research, which we discuss below, shows that unpaid household labor continues to make up a very substantial portion of total labor.

With incomplete contracting we expect a woman's bargaining power within the family to be inversely related to the labor market's premium on specific skills. As we have emphasized, women are generally at a disadvantage when competing for jobs with men because they are expected to leave the labor market for purposes of childbirth and child rearing.[13] Employers will therefore be more reluctant to invest in skills of women, and young women are likewise more reluctant to build up substantial employer-specific assets or even invest in the education that is needed for a specific skills kind of job since these may be forfeited with the birth of their first child.[14]

How great the motherhood disadvantage is, however, depends on the nature of skills that employers are seeking.[15] If such skills are highly specific to firms, or even to industries, and if a substantial part of training is paid by the employer, there is a strong disincentive to make these invest-ments in female employees when the average time horizon is compara-tively short. This is reinforced by women's own decisions because they are disinclined to invest in specific skills for which they are at a disadvantage. Even if a woman invests to acquire a specific skill, her investment will not be protected to the same degree as a man's. Women are therefore more likely than men to invest in general skills and/or in skills that are less prone to deteriorate when not used for some period of time. This implies a heav-ily gendered structure of educational choices, and it is not surprising that vocations with more general educational content and low atrophy rates—such as commerce, services, and home economics—are overwhelmingly female in composition.[16] Women facing tough labor market constraints may be better off aiming as high as possible in the marriage market and ed-ucating themselves in the "gracious arts" rather than in marketable skills.

In the Becker model, the difficulty of women finding paid work does not matter for the household division of labor so long as the productivity of the husband is greater. The household division of labor is always com-plete. The Becker model allows that women may have time left over to enter the labor market, especially during parts of the life cycle where there are no dependent children. But only the bargaining model implies that the amount of paid work, and the earnings power of the woman, will mat-ter for household division of labor. Also, insofar as skills are specific, paid employment should benefit men more than women because men are in a better position to accumulate specific skills.

The importance of the skill argument for understanding variation in bargaining dynamics inside the family is reinforced by broader cross-na-tional differences in the structure of production. Taking advantage of the international division of labor, some countries have specialized in the forms of production that use specific skills intensely while others have special-ized in production that uses general skills intensely.[17]

Note the irony of how welfare states, designed to protect the weak, may inadvertently hurt women in several ways. Wage compression increases the cost of child-care services. Protective institutions, such as high job security, seniority pay, and generous employer-financed benefits, tend to reinforce insider-outsider divisions, and since women are more likely to be outsiders, they are at a greater disadvantage compared to more flexible labor markets where low protection encourages investment in general skills. Labor unions, and the parties that represent them, may as a consequence be less likely to champion the cause of women and other outsiders. But even more important, labor market protections motivate both employers and employees to invest in employees' acquisition of firm-specific skills: firms because this is the way to get the most productivity out of their long-term obligations to employees, and workers because this is the path to advancement. Because firm-specific human capital depreciates with career interruptions, female labor market participation tends to be lower in countries with strong labor unions.[18]

In economies with fluid labor markets, by contrast, women are generally better able to compete on an equal footing with men in the labor market because investments in skills are mostly borne by workers rather than by employers. The general skills that are acquired through education do not depend on staying with a particular employer for a long period of time and do not lose value when the employee moves to a different employer.

Because of these differences in labor market institutions, the outside options of women in countries with fluid labor markets tend to be better than in specific skills systems, and by extension, so is their bargaining power within the family. This implies that, everything else being equal, female labor market participation tends to be lower in specific skills systems and the distribution of household work tends to be more unequal than in general skills systems.

Labor market effects, however, are mediated by social and economic policies deliberately designed to counter them. If governments support a woman's ability to form an independent household, especially through publicly provided services such as day care, and through employment for women in these services, they compensate for the exclusion of women from good jobs in the private labor market.[19] The Scandinavian countries are prime examples. They have attained high female participation rates by creating a large, and heavily feminized, public sector, as we discuss in more detail in chapter 6. This has been facilitated by frequent center-left governments where the interests of "outsiders" are effectively represented and reflected in public policies.

Empirical Analysis: Data and Measurement

To understand the effects of outside options on bargaining within the family, we took advantage of surveys of married and cohabitating couples undertaken by the International Social Survey Programme (ISSP) in 1994.[20] Based on answers to questions about household labor, we constructed a division of labor index. One of the questions in the survey, for example, reads: In your household who does the laundry, the washing and ironing? (1) Always the woman, (2) usually the woman, (3) about equal or both, (4) usually the man, (5) always the man. The other three questions ask who cares for sick family members, who shops for groceries, and who decides what is for dinner. One additional question asks who does repair work around the house. But such work is infrequent and often has a leisure or hobby component,[21] something that is confirmed by a principal factor analysis performed on all five items, which identifies two dimensions: one where only the first four items have high, and about equally large, factor loadings, and one where only the repair item has a moderately high loading.[22]

We base our division of household labor index on the first four items, where higher values mean that more of the work is performed by the woman. The factor loadings for each item are very similar (see note 22), so we use a simple additive index (weighting by the factor loadings makes no difference to the results). Since most household labor is done by the woman, one can loosely think of higher values as indicating more inequality in the division of labor. The variable ranges from 1 to 5, with 3 being an even sharing of work. The mean for the variable is 3.97, which is equivalent to an average response to each question of "usually the woman." None of the reported results change substantively if we instead use an index based on all five items.

The fact that child care is left out of these questions undoubtedly leads to a substantial understatement of the woman's share of work. Research on family work based on time diaries, which do include a category for child care, show that children of all ages increase women's overall unpaid work time three to four times more than they increase men's.[23] But we expect, at least, that the male-female division of child-care responsibilities will parallel the way they divide other family tasks.

Although it is not possible to know with precision how the survey-generated index (without child-care time) maps on to actual hours of work done, we can get a good sense of this by comparing the index to the results of international time budget research. According to one authoritative study, women on average perform more than two-thirds of total household work.[24] That study also shows that the average adult spends 230 minutes per day on domestic work, equivalent to 460 minutes, or almost 8 hours, for a household with two adults. If the answer "always the (wo)man" means that the (wo)man literally does all the work, the index's range of four units is equivalent to 460 minutes, or about 115 minutes per unit—or 14 hours per week—assuming equidistant spacing between the different values. One standard deviation on the index is then .67 or about 77 minutes of work a day, 9 hours per week. In the following we will assume that the index can be interpreted linearly in terms of time units, which seems reasonable and makes the substantive interpretation much more intuitive.

For paid work we use two variables that ask about the employment status of the respondent and of the spouse. It is coded 1 for those who are full-time employed, 0.5 for part-time employed, 0.25 for less than part-time employed, and 0 for those who consider themselves homemakers or who are retired. We ignore the unemployed and students. The variables are coded for men and women separately and are included as independent variables in the regressions of unpaid work. Since an average work week for a full-time worker is about 40 hours in most OECD countries, and about half that for a part-time worker, we may reasonably gauge the substantive meaning of results of this variable in terms of weekly hours (assuming a five-day working week).

To explain the individual-level variance in the division of labor, we use seven sets of independent variables. We measure the *(pretax) wage income* of the husband and wife separately, to gauge their effects on implicit bargaining over household work.[25] The *probability of divorce,* by our account, ought to affect the sensitivity of men and women to their economic circumstances.[26] *Past time spent on household labor* should have a negative effect on the acquisition of marketable skills and hence current outside options.[27] The *number of dependents* will tend to increase the total amount of household work, as well as increase the pressure, usually on the women, to specialize in such work.[28] *Education* is likely to boost labor force participation. In addition, families with highly educated spouses could be expected to share household duties more equitably. This could be seen as an effect of better outside long-term options not adequately captured by current employment and income, or one may speculate that education leads to more equitable gender norms.[29] *Religiosity* and *Catholicism* may also be factors of importance because they can be assumed to be related to perceptions of appropriate gender roles, and such roles are closely associated with the sexual division of labor.[30]

Age is also a variable of theoretical interest. Although information about age is only available for the respondent, the respondent's age is highly correlated with the age of the spouse and thus serves as a proxy for both. Age does not play any role in efficiency models, except insofar as it affects labor force participation through life-cycle effects or is associated with having dependent family members. We control for these variables directly. By contrast, age plays a role in bargaining models because it differentially affects the position of men and women in the remarriage market. As suggested above there are two reasons. First, the value of household-specific skills deteriorates with age because they are so closely related to the bearing and rearing of children. Second, age itself tends to be a liability in the remarriage market.

Since we do not have cohort data, we cannot exclude the possibility that age effects are due to generational differences. But if women in older generations are expected to assume more household labor because of gender norms, this should also show up as a positive effect of retirement on the female share of household work (controlling for labor market participation). The bargaining model would lead to the opposite prediction insofar as retirement marks a relative decline in males' outside options. We therefore include a *dummy for retirement*.

The final individual-level control is the *gender of the respondent* because there may be a tendency for people to exaggerate how much work they do in order to look better in the eyes of the interviewer. This could bias the results for other variables.

At the national level we focus on three variables: *part-time employment*, *skill specificity*, and *spending on public service provision*. Part-time employment is measured as the percentage share of the working-age population who are in part-time jobs.[31] The emphasis on specific as opposed to general skills in national training systems is measured by an index, which is equal to the mean, after standardization, of vocational training intensity and firm tenure rates.[32] Specific skill systems tend to undermine the employment opportunities of women. Yet, as we have argued, this gender bias can be reduced by deliberate policies to hire women to perform social and personal services through the public sector. Although there is no reason to think public service provision plays a role in general skill systems with flexible labor markets—public and private provision will be substitutes in this case—there is good reason to expect public service provision to reduce the labor market disadvantage of women in specific skills systems. The government is, in effect, creating a layer of general skills jobs in an economy where the private sector resembles a specific skills economy. We measure public service provision as government purchases of goods and services, net of government spending on defense, as a percentage of GDP. In practice, the bulk of nonmilitary purchases are social services.[33]

Empirical Estimation and Results

The division of household labor, if the theory is correct, is a function of individual-level characteristics (such as age or religiosity), family situation (such as the extent of caring responsibilities), as well as the availability of good "outside options" for spouses (essentially access to jobs and income). Outside options, in turn, vary across countries according to the availability of part-time employment, the skill system, public service provision, and the interaction of the latter two.[34] Yet since jobs and income are a reflection not merely of labor market conditions but also of individual preferences, caring responsibilities, and so on, these variables can be modeled as a function of both individual- and national-level variables. Consequently we use a multilevel modeling approach.[35] The model is explained in detail in appendix A. The detailed regression estimates are provided in tables 3.1 and 3.2. in appendix B. Here we focus on the substantive results.

The individual-level only results are shown in figure 3.1. As expected, the probability of divorce significantly decreases the female share of unpaid work. The effect is not large, but it has to be recalled that the measure is

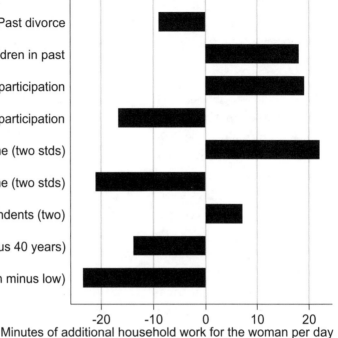

Figure 3.1. Individual-level determinants of the female share of household labor
Note: The effects are based on the regression results in model (2) in table 3.1 (see appendix B). The numbers are shown as projected effects on the weekly minutes of additional female household labor assuming that the reported share of female labor can be linearly translated into time units based on the results from time-budget studies (see text for details). All estimates are statistically significant at a .05 level (two-tailed) or better.

whether the respondent has been divorced in the past, which is only weakly (though positively) related to future divorce. Presumably worrying about, or at least being cognizant of, the possibility of a marriage breakup makes women inclined to assume a smaller share of household work and men more likely to accept this. As we will see shortly, higher divorce risk also makes women more prone to participate in paid employment.

Women who have sacrificed work for family in the past also end up with a greater share of the household workload in the present. Since this effect is estimated after controlling for the number of dependents presently in the household, it implies that past investments in household-specific skills is a major cause of the future gender division of labor. It also means that some of the effect of "the number of dependents" variable, which also somewhat disfavors the woman, will get magnified over time because of the implied loss of outside options, and hence bargaining power, as a result of investing in household-specific skills.

Unsurprisingly, labor force participation reduces the share of household work for both spouses, but more so for men. As we noted above, this is consistent with an interpretation that men are better able to take advantage of opportunities to acquire specific skills in the labor market. Note also that market income reduces the share of household work. In the Becker efficiency model the effect of market income on the division of household labor should be a step-function with a complete division of domestic labor always "in favor" of the spouse with the higher earnings power.[36] Thus the marginal effect of income for one spouse should be zero except at the point where it is equal, or close to equal, to that of the other spouse (when the marginal effect is then infinite).[37] In our data the male virtually always has more income, so female income should not matter for unpaid work; yet the effect is strong and continuous. It is easy to explain this finding in a bargaining model because bargaining power is continuous in external options (under the assumptions laid out in the appendix A).

Another consistent result is that age increases the share of household work performed by the woman. Since the result is for respondents of both genders, aging disproportionately affects women—a result that holds up when we run the regression for men and women separately.[38] The only possible explanation for this effect in an efficiency model is that age reduces labor market participation more for women than for men or that the scope of domestic work rises with age. Yet we have included controls for labor market participation and the number of dependents, and the effect of age is in fact *stronger* when these are included. In substantive terms, if we compare a newly wed couple at age twenty to a married couple at age forty, and controlling for everything else, the woman in the latter will spend about fourteen additional minutes a day on household work.[39]

As noted before, the effect of age is consistent with a bargaining perspective because age differentially affects men and women on the remarriage market. Yet it is also consistent with a generational hypothesis that younger generations have more equitable work norms. We cannot entirely exclude such an interpretation although it is noteworthy that the division of labor tends to be *more* equitable in families where the spouses are retired (the effect of the retirement variable is shown in table 3.1). Also, it is worth pointing out that *if* norms have changed over time, the bargaining model in fact has something to say about why, as we discussed in chapter 2. When outside options are important, and they *have* become more important over time in line with the rise in divorce rates, there is reason to expect that parents will raise their daughters to have more similar tastes for paid work as their sons. This makes daughters less willing to assume all domestic duties as adults. We consider this a fruitful area for future research.

Finally we note that education, as expected, is a strong predictor of more gender equality in the division of household work. Going from the lowest to the highest level of education reduces the predicted amount of household work by three hours a week. Note that this is after controlling for labor market participation and earnings, so it cannot simply be due to higher earnings power. When we run the regression separately for men and women it instead appears to be the result of a combination of better outside options for women and greater willingness of educated males to share work. The latter result again points to the role of values, which we will consider in a moment. It is also noteworthy that the results for paid work, which we discuss next (figure 3.2), show that education significantly raises labor force participation of both men and women. This has a knock-on effect on household labor.

We also controlled for religion (not shown), which tends to increase women's share of the household labor because women in religious families appear to be somewhat less likely to be in paid employment (see the results for paid work in table 3.2). Whether the measure is religiosity or Catholicism, however, these effects are small and rarely significant. We should not be surprised by this apparent lack of impact, even if religiosity is positively related to traditional gender norms. As we argued in chapter 2, norms are shaped by the same set of factors that affect bargaining power in the family and therefore do not necessarily have a strong direct effect.

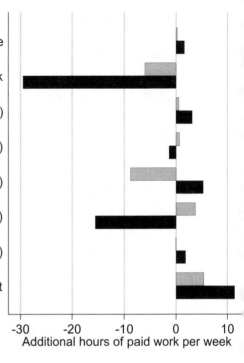

Figure 3.2. Multilevel determinants of the gender division of paid labor (males: top light-shaded bar; females: bottom black bar)
Note: The effects are based on the regression results in model (1) and (2) in table 3.2 (see appendix B). The numbers are shown as projected effects on the weekly hours of paid work assuming that the reported level of labor force participation can be linearly translated into hours and a full-time work week is forty hours. All estimates are statistically significant at a .05 level (two-tailed) or better.

The multilevel results in figure 3.2 are for paid employment for men and women separately (the full regression results are in the first half of table 3.2 in appendix B). The estimated effects are on the number of hours worked per week, assuming that a full-time job in the survey corresponds to a forty-hour work week. Not surprisingly given the previous results, past absence from the labor market to care for children has a strong negative effect on women's labor force participation. A woman who has taken off the maximum amount of time in the past for purposes of child rearing, as many do, almost ensures that she will not work later in life, whereas a woman who has not taken time off is predicted to work at least part time. By contrast, very few men exit the labor market to care for children (less than 16 percent), and when they do it tends to be for very brief periods (less than 2 percent in the sample have taken full-time leaves). This appears neither to much affect their subsequent participation in paid work nor to increase their share of household work. Indeed, a sensible interpretation of these results is that men take off work only to the extent that it does not hurt their careers.

The effects of age for paid employment are interesting to compare to those for household work. Excluding those who are retired, women increase their participation in the labor market as they age, whereas men substitute work for leisure. These are clearly life-cycle effects, but they imply that women are gaining some financial independence later in life, which we know from the results in figure 3.1 has the effect of reducing their share of household labor. In fact, this indirect effect of age essentially outweighs the adverse direct effect of age on the inequality in the division of household labor.[40] A reasonable interpretation is that aging reduces the value of women in the remarriage market but increases their value in the labor market. The net effect appears to be mildly positive, which is another reason to be skeptical of interpretations that stress the importance of generational differences in norms.

But the most interesting results in figure 3.2 concern the effects of the macrolevel variables. The gender division of labor, if our argument is right, should be affected by the interaction of skill specificity (which disadvantages women) and the size of the public sector (which compensates for such disadvantages). As we move from general to specific skill countries we expect women, but not men, to be increasingly disadvantaged in the labor market —except if the state steps in to provide jobs and services through the public sector. Such public employment policies, however, should not matter in general skills systems with flexible labor markets where they will simply replace private sector jobs for women. This is precisely the pattern we find.

When the public sector is small (zero on our standardized variable), the effect of skill specificity is to notably reduce the participation of women in paid work (the second to last bar). Going from the country with the most general skill system to the one with the most specific skill system—measured by the intensity of vocational training and length of firm tenure rates —reduces the predicted level of female participation in paid work by sixteen hours a week. Part of this effect, which is large, may be due to differences in preferences for work—and we would in fact expect work opportunities and preferences to be related as discussed in the next chapter—but it should be noted that we control for the incidence of part-time work, which does not usually rely on specific skills and therefore capture at least some of the national differences in preferences for labor market participation. Also, the dampening effect of specific skills on women's participation in paid work is attenuated by a large public sector, which is precisely what our production argument implies. Since the extent of public service provision does not matter when skill specificity is low (as shown in detail in appendix B, table 3.2), public sector employment appears to compensate for female disadvantages in private labor markets with heavy emphasis on specific skills.

The availability of part-time employment clearly also facilitates the entry of women into the labor market, and this is also true for men. In the case of male employment, however, skill specificity is not important. There is a hint in the full set of results (see table 3.2. in appendix B) that a large public sector may hurt the employment opportunities of men, but the effect is weak at best. If we think of public sector employment as providing a layer of general skills jobs, the conclusion is that skill systems are simply not important for the employment opportunities of men.

Figure 3.3 revisits the division of household labor but with the national-level variables standing in for the individual-level job and income variables (so that labor market opportunities are captured by differences in macroinstitutions). The complete regression results are in table 3.2 in appendix B. Consistent with the results for paid employment, women assume a larger share of household work in specific skills systems, but this inequality is attenuated by a larger public sector. The figure illustrates the estimated relationship between skill specificity and the household division of labor for different levels of public service provision. The y-axis shows the predicted female shares of household work when we assume a size of the public sector that corresponds to four groups of countries: (i) the United States,

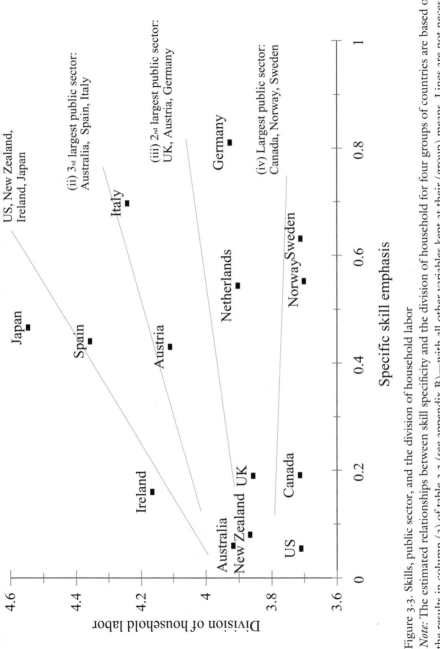

Figure 3.3. Skills, public sector, and the division of household labor

Note: The estimated relationships between skill specificity and the division of household labor for four groups of countries are based on the results in column (3) of table 3.2 (see appendix B)—with all other variables kept at their (group) means. Lines are not necessarily intersecting when the specific skill variable is o because each cluster has different mean values in the controls.

New Zealand, Ireland, and Japan with a small public sector, (ii) Australia, Spain, and Italy with the next smallest public sector, (iii) the United Kingdom, Austria, and Germany with intermediately sized public sectors, and (iv) Canada, Norway, and Sweden with large public sectors. We have also shown the actual location of all fourteen countries. Note how the trade-off between skill specificity and equality in the division of household labor is reduced by a larger public sector. In the countries with the largest public sector the trade-off disappears altogether. The only outlier is the Netherlands, which has a small public sector (it would belong to category i) but a fairly egalitarian division of labor. It appears that the Dutch achieve this outcome by having an exceptionally large and flexible market for part-time employment.

Conclusions

Explaining cross-national variation in income inequality has been one of the greatest preoccupations of modern political economy. But much of this analysis masks, we have argued, inequality within the very unit of analysis that is typically taken for granted: the family. When we abandon the traditional assumption of the family as a welfare maximizing unit, we confront the reality of strategic interaction between spouses. Because a spouse might favor his or her *share* of family welfare even at some expense of the *total* family welfare, it is important to disaggregate the family to understand the effects of labor market institutions and the public policies that govern them. Much distributive politics is "out of view" of standard political economy because it occurs inside the family where the division of labor and welfare does not enter official statistics. But the significance of family bargaining also "spills over" into the political contestation over public policies because the outside options in the household bargaining game are affected by these policies. As we will see in chapter 5 this produces a gender gap in partisan preferences.

In this chapter we examined how the assumption of family as a unit can lead us astray in understanding the household division of labor. First, we join a growing chorus of social scientists challenging the idea that the household division of labor reflects an efficient allocation of family resources.[41] A husband may resist his wife's outside employment, even if it could increase total family income (or more broadly, family utility including children's well-being), because her accumulation of market skills and experience broadens her exit options to the marriage. By ramping up her bargaining power within the marriage, this greater economic independence can result in the husband contributing more and receiving less in the way of unpaid work in the home. It probably also affects a long list of other matters that spouses have to agree on in their daily lives but that we do not have good data on—from what the family spends money on to how they spend time together.

Female labor force participation and higher female income do in fact shift the burden of household work a bit further onto men's shoulders. Furthermore, labor markets that put a premium on the accumulation of specific skills hurt women's ability to gain equality in household work. Because women in specific skills economies typically bear a bigger penalty for career interruptions, such as for child rearing, they face more limited work opportunities and may invest less in their market-relevant education as a result. This, in turn, weakens their bargaining power at home, and they get stuck sweeping floors more of the time than their counterparts in general skills economies.

Intriguingly, women in specific skills economies not only do a larger share of housework but also appear to do a larger share *over time*. This is because not only are their market skills low, but they deteriorate with time, dragging down women's outside options along the way. We doubt that most couples think explicitly in the terms we lay out here. But given the human propensity to slip into self-serving behavior, it is not at all unrealistic to suppose that spouses are quite aware of their options outside the marriage and sometimes test these. We ignore the strategic dimension of family life at the expense of realism and policy relevance.

Appendix A: Empirical Model

We take our point of departure in the general model presented in Steenbergen and Jones (2002):

$$(1)\ y_{ij} = \beta_{0j} + \sum_{p=1}^{P} \beta_{pj} x_{pij} + \varepsilon_{ij},$$

where y is the dependent variable, x is an explanatory variable, and i indexes individuals, j countries, and p variables. The dependent variable in our analysis is the gender division of household labor, and the first set of results refers to a model where the predictors are all individual-level variables, using country-specific intercepts (table 3.1).

The second set of results (the first two columns in table 3.2) separates out paid employment as a key "outside option" variable that is explained as a function of both national- and individual-level variables:

$$(2)\ x_{qij} = \gamma_{00} + \sum_{r=1}^{R} \gamma_{0r} z_{rj} + \sum_{s=1}^{S} \delta_{sj} x_{sij} + \delta_{ij},$$

where x_{qij} is the subset of individual-level variables measuring outside options (jobs and income in our setup), and z_{rj} are country-level predictors indexed by r—in our setup, part-time employment, skill system, public services, and the interaction of the latter two. In addition, there are S individual-level variables, X_{sij}, which are simply the remaining variables from (1) that are not measures of outside options. We focus on paid employment as the dependent outside option variable, although we could also have used market income.

Finally, we substitute equations (2) into (1) to get a model for y (the household division of labor) that is a function of both individual- and national-level variables. The advantage of doing this, compared to relying on individual-level variables only, is that we can examine how the gender division of household labor depends on national-level variables that shape outside options. This will also set the stage for the next section on the gender gap because it will make clear why men and women may have different preferences over policies that affect outside options. Specifically, the multilevel model for the household division of labor is

$$(3)\ y_{qij} = \mu_{0j} + \sum_{r=1}^{R} \mu_{0r} z_{rj} + \sum_{s=1}^{S} \phi_{sj} x_{sij} + \varsigma_{ij}.$$

Note that country-specific intercepts in equation (1) have been replaced by a single constant. In effect, equation (3) assumes that these intercepts are also a function of differences in the structure of labor markets captured by our national-level variables. This is a necessary assumption because the national-level variables are perfectly collinear with the intercepts and therefore cannot be entered simultaneously.

The effects of all independent variables are estimated using maximum likelihood regression with robust standard errors, assuming a normal density function for the disturbances. We obtained the estimates in STATA using the minimum likelihood procedure for survey data (countries are treated as clusters).

Appendix B: Regression Results

Table 3.1 shows the individual-level regression results for the household division of labor. Because much data for personal income are missing, the first column of table 3.1 excludes these variables while column (2) includes them. In column (3) we have omitted some variables in order to enable the inclusion of the Netherlands (to include Spain would also require omission of religiosity and the income variables). Regardless of specification, the results are similar, and figure 3.1. and the discussion in the main text focuses on the most complete set in column (2).

Table 3.2 shows the multilevel regression results for paid work for both genders, and then the results for the division of household labor (where the dependent variable is the female share of household work). The regression.model is described in appendix A. Note that while the substantive effects of the skill variable and its interaction with the size of the public sector are large in the case of women's work (both paid and unpaid), the standard errors are also very large. The reason is that there is strong collinearity between the public sector variable, the skill specificity variable, and the interaction term. We can easily circumvent this problem, however, by omitting the component public sector variable from the regression, which we have done in columns (1b), (2b), (3b), and (4b). We can do this without affecting any of the substantive results because the effect of the component public sector variable is zero, or close to zero, as we would indeed expect from the theory (when skills are general, public sector jobs simply substitute private sector jobs). Because there are virtually no effects on the estimated parameters for any other variables we have

Table 3.1. Individual-level determinants of the gender division of household work

	(1)	(2)	(3)
Divorce	−0.070***	−0.078**	−0.097***
	(0.021)	(0.028)	(0.031)
Past absence from paid work (women)	0.128***	0.157***	0.176***
	(0.036)	(0.040)	(0.044)
Male labor force participation	0.228***	0.166***	—
	(0.049)	(0.034)	
Female labor force participation	−0.172***	−0.145***	—
	(0.027)	(0.027)	
Male income (log)	—	0.054**	0.075**
		(0.018)	(0.020)
Female income (log)	—	−0.053***	−0.057***
		(0.014)	(0.016)
Number of dependents	0.019*	0.031**	—
	(0.010)	(0.013)	
Age	0.006***	0.006***	0.002**
	(0.001)	(0.001)	(0.001)
Education	−0.026***	−0.034***	−0.041***
	(0.008)	(0.010)	(0.011)
Retired	−0.050	−0.082	−0.087***
	(0.059)	(0.051)	(0.025)
Religiosity	0.006	0.005	0.014*
	(0.009)	(0.010)	(0.007)
Catholic	0.059**	0.033	0.012
	(0.019)	(0.029)	(0.033)
Gender of respondent (female)	0.206***	0.209***	0.214***
	(0.036)	(0.043)	(0.035)
N	5719	3570	4939
No. of countries	12	12	13

Notes: Entries are maximum likelihood estimates with standard errors in parentheses. All models include country-specific intercepts (not shown).

Key: ***p < .01; **p < .05; *p < .10 (two-tailed test)

Table 3.2. Multilevel determinants of the gender division of labor

	Paid work				Household work (female share)			
	Women (1)	(1b)	Men (2)	(2b)	(3)	(3b)	(4)	(4b)
Divorce	0.042* (0.016)		0.007 (0.017)		−0.098** (0.028)		−0.134** (0.029)	
Past absence from paid work	−0.737** (0.045)		−0.152** (0.035)		0.184** (0.031)		0.203** (0.049)	
Number of dependents	−0.017* (0.009)		0.008* (0.004)		0.043** (0.008)		—	
Age	0.004** (0.001)		−0.011** (0.001)		0.006** (0.001)		0.005** (0.001)	
Education	0.022** (0.006)		0.016** (0.004)		−0.032** (0.006)			
Religiosity	−0.020** (0.006)		−0.005 (0.004)		0.003 (0.010)		—	
Catholic	0.014 (0.018)		−0.017 (0.021)		0.054 (0.040)		0.028 (0.047)	
Retired	—		—		−0.152** (0.037)		−0.137** (0.047)	
Gender of respondent (female)	−0.002 (0.018)		−0.171** (0.015)		0.219** (0.037)		0.209** (0.027)	
Public sector	0.013 (0.208)	—	−0.102 (0.057)	—	−0.057 (0.394)	—	0.069 (0.595)	—
Skill specificity	−0.389* (0.187)	−0.4** (.10)	−0.002 (0.073)	0.08 (.07)	0.876* (0.432)	0.9** (.30)	0.851 (0.542)	0.8** (.30)
Public sector × skill specificity	0.690 (0.431)	0.7** (.12)	0.134 (0.154)	−0.06 (.11)	−1.302 (0.840)	−1.4** (.46)	−1.469 (1.108)	−1.3** (.46)
Part-time employment	0.019** (0.004)		0.009** (0.003)		−0.004 (0.012)		−0.025** (0.006)	
N	5312		3045		7144		9520	
No. of countries	12		12		12		14	

Note: Entries are maximum likelihood estimates; standard errors in parentheses.

Key: **p < .01; *p < .05

omitted these results. The only change is that the standard errors on the skill specificity variable and its interaction with public sector are notably reduced. So the effect of skill specificity and its interaction with public sector can in fact be estimated quite precisely.

Column (4) omits variables from the regression that allow both the Netherlands and Spain to be included, but doing so has an effect only on part-time employment, which has a greater impact (mainly due to the Netherlands).

4

FERTILITY

As women have moved inexorably into the paid workforce over the past century, fertility rates have plummeted. Average OECD fertility dropped from 2.4 children per woman in 1970 to less than 1.7 in 2000, during which time the female labor force participation rate rose from 45 percent to more than 65 percent. Juxtaposing these figures against time on the x-axis produces the figure of a giant X, as shown in figure 4.1.

One also finds this X in cross-sectional depictions of fertility and female labor force participation where countries are sorted on the x-axis by GDP or level of development. The reasons for the inverse relationship between women's workforce participation and fertility are not hard to fathom: women's opportunity costs of staying at home rise with the possibilities for remunerative work outside the home. And as we have argued, when the gender division of labor declines, divorce rates increase, and women will have strong insurance and bargaining incentives to shun heavy investment in household-specific assets. Below-replacement fertility may just be a fact of the modern world.

The inverse relationship between women's paid work and fertility for rich democracies has weakened, however, in recent years. While female labor force participation has everywhere risen, and fertility everywhere declined, the rates of change vary. For some countries the right leg of the X juts out in a jaunty pose, defying gravity. In fact, if we look at the cross-national pattern, the relationship has reversed, as shown in figure 4.2. Whereas in 1970 there was a clear and fairly strong negative relationship

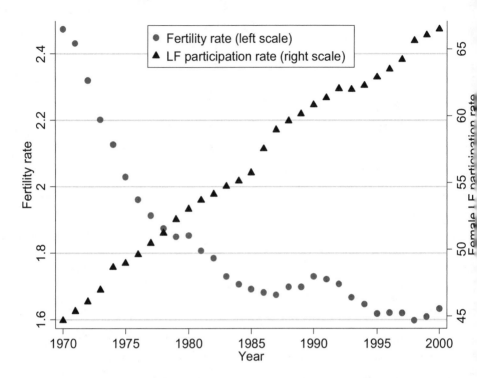

Figure 4.1. Fertility and female labor force participation rate (OECD average)

between female labor force participation and fertility (see panel a), in 2002 the relationship is *positive* (panel b). What explains this puzzle?

One frequently cited answer is that gender-friendly government policies that make it easier for women to balance family and career can stem or even reverse the decline in fertility (Esping-Andersen 1999; McDonald 2000). But this is hardly the whole story, as we can see from the substantial variation in fertility that government subsidies of child care and other family services leaves unexplained (see figure 4.3).

This scatter plot suggests that variation in child-care spending has less bearing on fertility levels than one might expect (r = .13). Our examination of labor market structures reveals why. First, in countries with highly flexible labor markets, affordable day care services tend to be available through the market, and women can relatively easily find jobs that can pay

---

Figure 4.2. (opposite) The reversal of the relationship between female labor force participation and fertility, 1970 and 2002

1970

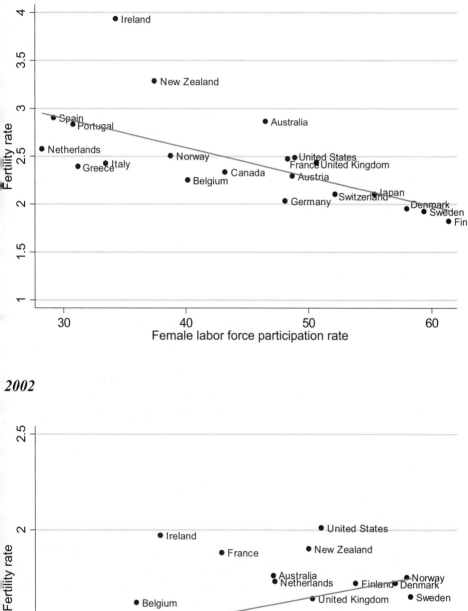

2002

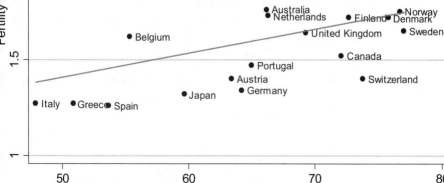

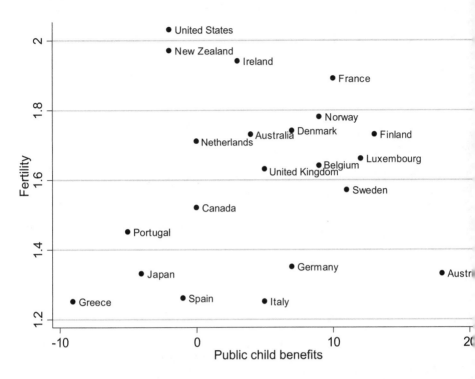

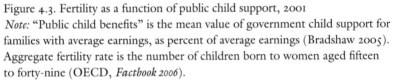

Figure 4.3. Fertility as a function of public child support, 2001
Note: "Public child benefits" is the mean value of government child support for
families with average earnings, as percent of average earnings (Bradshaw 2005).
Aggregate fertility rate is the number of children born to women aged fifteen
to forty-nine (OECD, *Factbook 2006*).

for these services (United States and New Zealand stand out in the figure).
Publicly provided services in these countries will only have an effect at the
very low end of the wage scale. Second, government subsidies for child
care and other family work provide only a partial explanation: increasing
women's ability to supply their labor will be of limited effect in labor markets organized around long-term contracts and specific investments in
human capital that make career interruptions costly to the employer. Austria, Germany, and Italy, for example, have generous subsidies for families
with children yet exhibit low fertility rates. As we have argued, as long as

women are more likely than men to take time off to rear children or take care of sick and aging family members, females are actuarially more costly employees than their male counterparts. The resulting "statistical discrimination" need not be buttressed by unflattering gender stereotypes to be devastating to women's employment opportunities.

To be sure, publicly provided day care helps reduce the problem because it shortens career interruptions and gives women more flexibility in balancing work and career. But child care does not eliminate the problem because women are still more likely than men to leave work for childbirth and for caring for sick children or elderly parents. In jobs where there is a premium on continuous careers, this means that employers are less likely to invest in the human capital of women. In response, women shift their career investment toward (more general skills) occupations with high job flexibility. Where those jobs are in short supply, the desire of women to have active careers forces them to sacrifice family by having fewer children. The only effective way to deal with this problem, we argue, is for the state to create or subsidize jobs that are highly flexible in terms of hours and career interruptions. This conclusion reserves a large role for government intervention, a role we suggest is warranted and indeed required to address the large distributional consequences of social norms that underwrite the traditional sexual division of labor.

Females have been drawn into the paid labor market in growing numbers. As we showed in chapter 3, the shift to postindustrial economies has increased the demand for female labor by lowering the male brawn premium and lowering the costs of career interruption. In many countries, moreover, an increased risk of divorce gives women an additional reason to invest in market skills as a hedge against post-divorce poverty and a weak bargaining position in the family in the meantime (Edlund and Pande 2002). In still other countries where neither the labor market is women-friendly enough to serve as a pull nor divorce laws are lax enough to push women into the labor market for insurance against poverty in the event of divorce, we find evidence of a demonstration effect. When forced to choose between staying at home to have babies or straining against intimidatingly heavy and low glass ceilings, women in these countries are increasingly opting for the latter because they see women elsewhere succeeding professionally. Indeed, these are the countries with the lowest fertility in our sample because low divorce tends to be associated with a heavily male-dominated labor market.

Women and the Labor Market

In chapter 3 we suggested that two factors are critical in accounting for the dramatic increase in female labor force participation in the postwar decades. First, the rise of the service sector has drawn women into the workforce in great numbers. Second, higher divorce rates appear to have motivated many women to earn their own income as a hedge against postdivorce poverty. But even in countries where neither of these pull-and-push factors is present to a similar degree, women seem to be cuing off the behavior of women elsewhere. There is nothing irrational about this in the sense that the fact that women in other developed countries can and do have careers suggests that this should be possible elsewhere as well. Although their behavior may seem maladapted to their incentive structures, their collective reduction in fertility is also raising alarm in governments around the world about the impending pension crisis or immigration headache as the indigenous workforce continues to shrink. Even if more for fiscal concerns than for female welfare, the fertility bust is forcing governments to think of ways to help women better balance family and career.

Demand for Female Labor

If the industrial revolution's labor-saving devices made it possible for women to compete more equally with men, the service sector has even more dramatically reduced the advantages of male size and muscle power. In addition to the drop in the male brawn premium, another factor contributes to the striking correlation between the proportion of the service sector in a nation's economy and the rate of female labor force participation (recall figures 2.1. and 2.3). Many service sector jobs require general rather than specific skills, resulting in a smaller liability from a woman's difficulty in committing to long, uninterrupted tenure.

Firms get lower returns on human capital investment in the sorts of service sector jobs where learning by doing and accumulated experience are less vital to labor productivity. Notice that the specificity of skill is a separate matter from the level of skill. A nurse, for example, may be highly skilled, but a nurse's skills are fairly general, mobile across hospitals, and likely to remain valuable following a few years' break from the workplace. This contrasts with many manufacturing jobs in coordinated market economies, where each industry and even each firm has its own production and management techniques in which constant and small adjustments are an integral part of competitive firm strategy.[1] Females, given the expectation of their work discontinuity on account of family work, are less valuable to employers that make use of specific skills to increase labor productivity (Estévez-Abe 1999, Estévez-Abe et al. 2001).

The demand for female labor has therefore grown with the rise of general skills jobs in the service sector that do not penalize employees who are not expected to stay on the job beyond a few years. Liberal market economies have deindustrialized relatively quickly because labor markets are unprotected and firms are free to move out of manufacturing or relocate manufacturing operations overseas in pursuit of cheaper labor. At the same time, deregulated labor markets have allowed wages and prices to drop quickly in lower-productivity services. Coordinated market economies, by contrast, have developed modes of production around long-term, specific investments in human capital, which, together with wage-setting systems that have kept skilled wages relatively low, have had the consequence that manufacturing remains a larger proportion of the overall private sector economy. In addition, the high employment protection and compression of wages that is associated with specific skill production has significantly retarded the expansion of jobs in personal and social services, which tend to rely on flexibility and often low wages (Iversen 2005). This has pushed wages and prices up in services.

Figure 4.4 illustrates the pattern. It shows domestic price levels, which are largely a function of wages and prices in nontraded service, on the x-axis, and employment in low productivity services—retail, wholesale, hotels, and restaurants (RWHR)—as a share of total employment in RWHR and manufacturing on the y-axis.[2] With the exception of Ireland (which has relatively centralized wage bargaining), the liberal market economies cluster at one end (smaller circle), exhibiting low price levels and a high share of RWHR employment, and the opposite patterns holds for coordinated market economies (larger circle).

As we discuss in more detail below, among coordinated market econo-

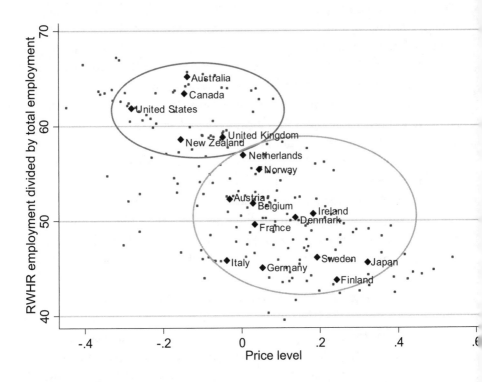

Figure 4.4. Prices and employment in retail, wholesale, hotels, and restaurants (RWHR) as share of manufacturing employment, 1990s
Note: The price level is the log of the inverse of the real exchange rate, using the U.S. dollar as the reference currency, *minus* the effect of GDP/capita on the real exchange rate. Positive values imply higher prices on nontraded goods relative to the U.S. dollar.

mies, Scandinavia is an exception in total service employment because of a large public service sector. Governments in these countries have also taken a more active role in reallocating labor across sectors through active labor market policies.[3]

Divorce Risk

Compared to a 14.6 percent average divorce rate for OECD countries in 1970, nearly one in two marriages ended in divorce by 2005. Against the background of high divorce levels, we expect that women are more likely to enter the workforce, holding constant demand for female labor. Unable to rely on marriage as an insurance against poverty, more women in high-divorce societies will "self insure" by earning an income on their own.

The high correlation—0.9—between divorce rates and female labor force participation rates fairly screams a causal connection, but note that the causal arrow can go the other way as well: two-career families are not taking full advantage of gains from division of labor, which means that the noneconomic benefits from the marriage have to be larger to sustain those families. As the outside options of women improve, the bargaining space inside the marriage shrinks. Economically self-sufficient women can abandon marriage without the economic hit that dependent women would have to endure, leaving fewer marriages to survive those utility calculations. There is nothing cynical about this observation because it implies that fewer women are trapped in bad marriages for economic reasons (whereas good ones persist).

Demonstration Effects

Demand for female labor and increased divorce risks are demonstrable factors in female labor market entry. More puzzling is why women try so hard to enter the workforce in countries where the demand for female labor is low and where divorce is relatively hard and rare. In those countries, notably Ireland, Italy, Japan, Portugal, Spain, and Korea, women seem to be responding to hostile labor markets not by giving up on career prospects and settling for a traditional motherhood role, but by trying even harder at the expense of childbirth. These countries have among the lowest female labor force participation rates in the OECD, but their fertility rates are also at the bottom of the charts.

Demonstration effects are related to the broader question of cultural change or the evolution of stereotypes. In chapter 2 we argued that parents adjust their socialization and investment strategies depending on whether females can secure a better livelihood by marrying well or educating themselves for remunerative careers of their own. Demonstration effects are an interesting subset of value change in that females may not only be unwilling to stay within inherited norms when opportunities for advancement present themselves, but they may be unwilling to wait for those opportunities before trying to secure them anyway. Another way to phrase this is that women's expectations about what career opportunities they can reasonably expect to have in the labor market are influenced by the opportunities they observe women having in other countries. Media exposure to high profile women in other societies may make women impatient for similar opportunities for professional success, providing an inspiration to strive harder for workplace advancement than the objective incentives would seem to warrant. Contrary to the "opportunity cost thesis," in which opportunities for remunerative work translate straightforwardly into less time for babies, fertility among developed nations is positively related to ease of employment and career advancement for women.

Data and Measurement

We model fertility as a function of individual traits, for example, age and education, sectoral differences (occupational group, public versus private), and macrovariables at the country level, such as the economy's predominant skill system and the level of public service provision.[4] The individual-level data are from most recent Luxembourg labor force surveys (LES), which are from the late 1990s or 2000, with the exception of the Nordic countries where the latest available surveys are from 1990. Among the rich democracies, on which we focus, there are microdata for thirteen countries: Austria, Belgium, Britain, France, Germany, Greece, Ireland, Netherlands, Norway, Spain, Sweden, Switzerland, and the United States (Canada and Finland had to be excluded because of lack of data on fertility). We complement these microdata with macrodata for twenty OECD countries for a thirty-one-year period running from 1970 through 2000.[5] Although we cannot test individual- or sector-level hypotheses with these data, the much larger number of country-year observations allows us to draw more definite inferences about the effects of macroinstitutions and policies, and they also permit us to explore the idea that fertility behavior in one country is affected by female labor force participation in other countries ("demonstration effects").

For the microdata we focus on fertility among women aged eighteen to forty-five but compare the results to men. For these data fertility is measured as the number of children in the respondent's household.[6] Although this number includes children born to women other than the respondent, the error will be small and is unlikely to be systematically related to any explanatory variable. The average number of children per woman in our sample is slightly above 1, whereas we know from the macrodata that women in these countries on average have 1.7 children at the time of the surveys. The simple reason for this discrepancy is that we are examining a cross section of women at different ages. To facilitate the interpretation of the results we multiply the estimated effects by 1.6 to get numbers that are comparable to the standard definition of fertility (average number of children born to each woman).

At the individual level we use sector of employment and occupation as the key independent variables. Sector refers to whether the respondent is employed in the public or private sector, whereas occupation refers to ILO's ISCO-88 classification at the 1-digit level. The idea is that the trade-off between career and family is less steep for women employed in the public sector and in occupations relying on general skills and flexible employment contracts. Occupations requiring highly specific skills and full-time commitments should not be conducive to balancing work and family. Note that the effect on fertility (if any) could be either a result of women in particular occupations responding to a steeper trade-off by having fewer children, or it could be a result of women with less intense preferences for children self-selecting into occupations where this is a comparative advantage. Both mechanisms are consistent with our political economy argument, and we would not expect either to be of particular salience for men since they are rarely primary caretakers.[7]

We have two microlevel indicators of whether jobs are conducive to women combining work and family. The first is the incidence of part-time employment; the other is the skill specificity of particular occupations. Part-time employment is simply the share of respondents who say they are in part-time jobs. Skill specificity is an individual-level variable based on the ISCO-88 occupational classification coupled with labor force data. It measures the specialization of skills in different occupations, following Iversen and Soskice (2001) and Cusack, Iversen, and Rehm (2006).[8]

At the macrolevel we distinguish between countries with production systems that emphasize specific skills and long job tenures and hence tend to "penalize" women for having children. As in the previous chapter, we measure these differences by an index that combines information on average firm tenure rates and vocational training activity.[9] Because both workers and employers want to reap the long-term benefits of specific skills investments, and because workers with such skills will find it harder to move around, firm tenure rates tend to be longer for workers with highly specific skills. Vocational training does not necessarily imply greater attachment to individual firms, but such training nevertheless represents investments in human capital that are more specific to particular jobs than those acquired through general education. Such investments again place a premium on continuous careers, and children interfere with such continuity. Combining firm tenure rates and vocational training activity gives a good summary measure of salient differences in national skill systems.[10]

While economies that rely heavily on specific skills are likely to have steeper trade-offs between work and family for women, this effect is attenuated by deliberate policies aimed at reducing the effect. As many countries in Europe experience growing fiscal strains as a result of low fertility and an aging population, active family policies are likely to become more important—not just as a response to political demands, but also as an economic imperative. The key for the success of such policies in today's world is not that they subsidize families with children—a strategy that, as noted, has met with limited success when attempted—but rather that they empower women to pursue careers without having to sacrifice family. This means spending on high-quality, full-time child care, and the creation, or subsidization, of flexible, general skills jobs in the public sector.[11]

Findings

Detailed regression results are presented in tables 4.1 (for the microdata) and 4.2 (for the macrodata) in appendix A. At the individual level the results confirm some well-established facts about the determinants of fertility. First, fertility rises with age at a progressively slower rate until the equilibrium number of children is reached—a number that depends on the other variables in the equation such as family status and education. Second, singles not surprisingly have fewer children than married couples, and, third, a long education also reduces fertility—about 200 fewer children for every 1,000 women with a high education (compared to women

with a low education). The education effect is partly because a long education delays the time of the first child, and partly because the opportunity
costs of having children rise with education. It is notable in our results,
however, that the effect of education is similar for men, despite the fact
that men rarely assume the role as primary caretakers and consequently
face a smaller career penalty from having children. We surmise that people with high education pursue a different "investment" strategy in their
offspring than those with low education. It is a well-known fact that there
is a strong class bias in higher education, and this may reflect the fact that
highly educated parents spend more time and financial resources to ensure the educational success of their children. The likely consequence is
that more effort will be concentrated on fewer children.

While age and education impact fertility in a similar way for men and
women, this is not true for sector of employment or occupation. What is
immediately apparent from these results is that occupation or sector of
employment makes little difference for men, whereas for women it is quite
important. Among 1,000 women in the public sector, we find en estimated
70 more children than among 1,000 women in the private sector, controlling for age, education, and marital status. This translates into a predicted higher fertility rate of 112 (since the actual number of children
among women aged eighteen to forty-five has to be multiplied by 1.6 to
get a comparable fertility rate). In contrast, among men there a slightly
negative effect of public sector employment on their number of children
(though it is not significant). Overall, the differences in the number of
children among men in different sectors and occupations are small and do
not display any systematic pattern, which suggests that they capture differences in the composition of the labor force of each occupation that our
control variables fail to capture. If so, we can get a more accurate picture
of the effect of occupation on female fertility by subtracting the estimated
numbers for men from the estimated numbers for women. In other words,
we use the number of children among males in each sector/occupation as
a reference to gauge the net effect of sector and occupation on female fertility. In the case of public sector employment, the net effect of employment in this sector (as opposed to the private sector) is to raise the number
of children for females by 89, which translates into a predicted gain in the
fertility rate of 142. This is shown as the top black bar in figure 4.5.

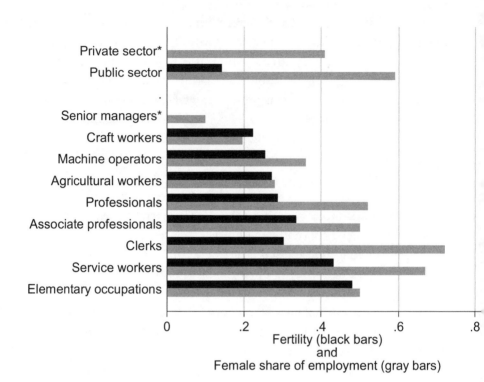

Private sector*
Public sector

Senior managers*
Craft workers
Machine operators
Agricultural workers
Professionals
Associate professionals
Clerks
Service workers
Elementary occupations

0   .2   .4   .6   .8

Fertility (black bars)
and
Female share of employment (gray bars)

Reference groups

Figure 4.5. Occupation, fertility, and female employment
Note: Fertility is the estimated additional number of children per woman in a particular sector (private sector is reference group) or occupation (senior managers is the
reference group), assuming that women aged eighteen to forty-five will eventually
end up with the average number of children per woman in the thirteen countries for
which we have labor force surveys (1.6 times the number of actual children in the
surveyed eighteen to forty-five age group). The estimates are based on the results in
model (1) and (2) in table 4.1 in appendix A. These estimates control for age (plus
age squared), family status (single), and education (medium and high compared to
low). To control for unobserved characteristics of workers in each sector and occupation we measure number of children among women relative to the number of
children among men in each sector/occupation. The occupations are ordered from
top to bottom so that the incidence of part-time employment is increasing.

This number may not seem particularly striking, but it is important to keep in mind that public sector jobs include both civil servants and workers employed in welfare services. The former type of public sector job is found everywhere and is not likely to be particularly conducive to combining career and family. Indeed, career bureaucrats have traditionally been men working full time in a hierarchical organizational structure that rewards seniority and hence the accumulation of long tenures. The public sector jobs that have come to be dominated by women, and offer much more flexibility, emerged only with the rise of the welfare state, although the extent to which this is true varies a great deal across countries.[12] We have more to say about this below. For now simply keep in mind that the effect of public sector employment covers very different types of workers (from senior civil servants to day care workers).

Using the same methodology for the occupations, which cover both the private and the public sector, and using fertility among senior managers as the reference group, the other black bars in figure 4.5 show the estimated fertility rates among women in different occupations (again relative to men in those occupations). Estimates are all above the 0-line, which means that women always have more children in these occupations than in senior management. The occupations have been ordered from top to bottom so that they exhibit increasing levels of part-time employment, which is also correlated with the share of women in each occupation (which are shown by gray bars). Part-time employment is a measure of employment flexibility, and it is also closely related to the specificity of human capital investments required in different occupations, so moving from top to bottom in the graph entails increasing the general skills intensity of jobs.

From this it is apparent that fertility is notably higher in general skills occupations with a high incidence of part-time employment—especially service and sales workers and elementary occupations. The estimated average fertility rate for women in these sectors is .456, or 456 children per 1,000 women, higher than for women who are in higher managerial positions. Since these are also the occupations that disproportionately employ women, the explanation for sector differences in fertility is clearly related to the explanations of labor market gender segmentation. Agriculture turns out to be a bit of an outlier if we examine the results for men and women separately (see table 4.1 in appendix A) since it turns out that both men and women in this sector have more children than what one might expect from the nature of agricultural production, which hardly offers a lot of employment flexibility. It is tempting to explain this as a result of more traditional family values in the countryside, as we suggested in chapter 2.

The rest of our regression analysis adds country-level variables for type of labor market and amount of government spending to gauge the effects of macrolevel variables (see model 3 and 4 of table 4.1 in the appendix). We also use these variables in a separate macrodata set that includes a larger number of countries (nineteen as opposed to thirteen) and time series for the period 1970–2000. The results from these regressions are in table 4.2 of the appendix.

We focus on the role of skill system and government consumption, and because these vary across countries only, we omit the (perfectly collinear) country-specific intercepts in the microdata (the macrodata actually allow more flexibility as discussed below). In effect, we assume that these intercepts are a function of differences in the macrolevel institutional variables. Insofar as this assumption is tenable, the results show that countries with production systems that rely on specific skills have lower fertility rates than countries with production systems that rely more on general skills. In our thirteen-country sample, going from the country with the most general skills system (United States) to the one with the most specific (Belgium) reduces the number of children by about 160 for every 1,000 women. But the effect for men is actually the opposite, although not as strong (about 90 *more* children).

At first blush this difference between men and women seems puzzling but the explanation turns out to be quite simple. The reason is that male respondents are in large part recording the choices of their spouses, who may or may not be working. Female respondents, on the other hand, are all working at least part time. If we compare working and nonworking women of childbearing age, it turns out, unsurprisingly, that the latter have 270 more children per 1,000 women (these are for the eighteen to forty-five age group sample). Hence, the positive effect of specific skills systems for men shows that female labor force participation is relatively low in these systems, and that male respondents therefore are more likely to be married to women who are not working and who have more children.

Nevertheless, the net effect of specific skills systems is to notably reduce overall fertility, which is clearly evident in the twenty country macrosample if we use actual fertility rates as the dependent variable (column 1 in table 4.2 of Appendix A). Assuming that government consumption and all other variables are kept at their average, specific skills systems reduce fertility rate by about 0.45 (again using the United States–Belgium comparison), which is a large effect.[13] This difference is partly offset, however, if we consider that many specific skill systems have large public sectors. In fact, government consumption, or public provision of services, greatly reduces the adverse effects of specific skills systems on fertility. When the public sector is as large as in the Scandinavian countries, there is no significant effect on fertility of the skill system at all.

The role of government spending can be further detailed from the multilevel results. At relatively low levels of spending most dollars will go to pay the salaries of career bureaucrats who keep the wheels of the state apparatus running. As noted above, these tend to be males in long-term employment, and there is no reason that such spending should have any beneficial effects for women—quite to the contrary. At higher levels of spending, however, more resources will go into the provision of social services (day care, care for the elderly, schools, hospitals, and so on), which tend to entail more female employment on more flexible terms. The effect of public employment on fertility is therefore contingent on the level of government spending, and we capture this by including a cross-level interaction between sector of employment (at the individual level) and government consumption (at the national level).

Figure 4.6 shows the estimated individual-level effect of public employment at different levels of public consumption (the straight black line). At low levels of spending, the effect of public employment is actually to reduce fertility among women. Presumably women who compete for jobs in the civil service cannot afford also to have large families. But as government spending rises, the effect of public employment becomes positive—presumably because jobs are increasingly in public services where the career-family trade-off is less steep.

The figure also shows the aggregate effects of government consumption on fertility, assuming that spending as a percentage of GDP is proportional to the share of the workforce employed in the public sector (the

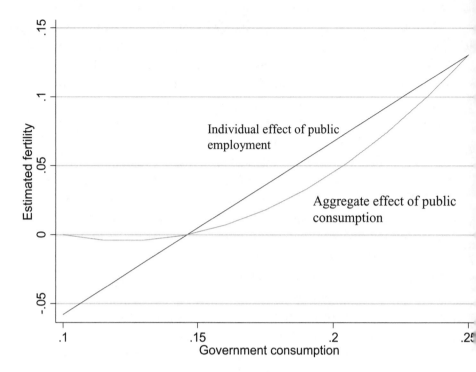

Figure 4.6. Government consumption (share of GDP) and fertility
Note: Based on Model (3) in Table 4.1 of Appendix A

curved line). At first more spending has a (slightly) negative effect as more women take up civil service jobs, but at around 15 percent of GDP (approximately the level in Ireland) the effect of additional spending is to raise fertility, and at the highest recorded level of spending (Sweden), predicted fertility is about 200 children per 1,000 women higher (after adjusting for the fact that we are measuring average number of children in a cross sample rather than actual fertility rates). In the macroregression the number is 270 children for a country with an average score on the skill variable. If we take into account the negative effect of increased female labor force participation, the number is similar to the one for the microdata—about 180—which is still large enough to lift many low fertility countries in Europe above the threshold for population sustainability. And, again, the large adverse effects of specific skills systems on fertility are nearly eliminated with a large public sector.

On balance, it is clear that for working women a large public sector is associated with higher fertility. As more and more women want to have careers, facilitating their ability to do so without making large sacrifices in terms of family is therefore the best bet to raise fertility rates to the sustainable population equilibrium. In countries such as Germany this may not seem like an obvious solution because the German state bureaucracy has been so dominated by predominantly male civil servants. A service-based welfare state works according to a completely different logic.

It is still true that female entry into paid employment is associated with a decline in fertility rates, but interestingly enough governments cannot avoid this even if they somehow managed to keep women at home. Not only do policies that make it hard for women to participate in the labor market cause them to reduce, rather than increase, the number of children, but higher female participation rates in neighboring countries seem to have a similar effect as higher female participation in the country in question. In the macroresults (table 4.2) this shows up when we include a variable for average female labor market participation in foreign countries while simultaneously controlling for domestic female labor market participation rates. To exclude the possibility that the "external" labor force participation rate picks up common shocks that affect all countries simultaneously, we also include a full set of time dummies. With this setup, the results indicate that a 10 percent increase in the average foreign fertility rate has the predicted effect of reducing the domestic fertility rate by about 0.55. This is a large effect and is in fact about ten times greater that the effect of a similar change in the domestic labor force participation rate. But recall that the external fertility rate is always an average of nineteen countries (the twenty countries in the sample minus the country observed), which implies that the effect of a change in the participation rate in any single foreign country is only about half that of a similar domestic change.

Even if we allow for the possibility that some of this effect is reflecting unobserved variables—although the relationship is highly robust to different model specifications—what this suggests to us is that women do cue off the behavior of women elsewhere. If women in Scandinavia are able to have careers, women in Germany appear to conclude that they can too, and they take the necessary steps to make it possible—especially by having fewer children. This cross-national network effect clearly makes it very difficult for any government to pursue policies that keep women at home.

At least this cannot be done without notable adverse effects on the fertility rate and hence the future funding of the welfare state.

Labor Markets and Fertility: The Cases of the United States, Japan, Germany, and Sweden

The quantitative results of the previous section suggest that gender-friendly labor markets promote fertility, and that public sector spending can generate a demand for female labor when the private sector is otherwise hostile on account of a premium on continuous careers to which females cannot commit. In this section we narrow our focus to a few country cases to check the logic suggested by the aggregate analysis.

Sweden and the United States, so unlike in many respects, both have relatively high fertility by the standards of rich democracies, and we have provided an argument for why this is so. The general skills nature of the U.S. economy gives firms less reason to discriminate against women in the expectation that they will interrupt their careers for family work. Although the Swedish manufacturing sector is organized around specific skills, the large size of its public sector has created an enormous pool of general skills jobs to which women have flocked. Although the demand for female labor was generated differently in the two countries, the effect in both countries is the same, to relieve women of the need to expend extra effort to succeed in the workplace. In Germany and Japan, where the workplace is less naturally conducive to female success, females in large numbers have shown themselves willing to forgo childbearing rather than to give up on remunerative work. The result is stunningly low rates of aggregate fertility.

Female labor force participation rates in the four countries in 1961 were not strikingly different, nor were their rates of fertility. By 1990, however, Sweden and the United States had significantly outpaced Germany and Japan in both. In the United States, the service sector economy has driven the rise in female labor force participation. Clerical jobs not only drew in ever larger numbers of women into the workforce, but they also heightened women's educational aspirations, which in turn allowed subsequent generations of women to move into other areas of the economy.[14] The narrowing of the male-female wage gap since 1980 has been attributed to the narrowing of the education gap.[15]

The important influence of clerical sector expansion on the American married women's labor force participation contrasts with the Japanese experience, where expansion of clerical work, and the service sector more generally, has not linked to an exponential growth in female labor force involvement.[16] Much clerical work in Japan remains embedded in career ladders in internal labor markets open only to men.[17] Although Japanese employers are not required by law to maintain long-term labor contracts as in many European welfare states, top tier Japanese firms have organized corporate structure and competitive strategies around competition for scarce labor. Lifetime employment and seniority advancement, labor market practices that may sound culturally quaint, were adaptations to rapid economic growth after World War II when hitching one's career to a firm made good economic sense. The consequences for females, though unintended, were dramatic. Females were considered a bad employment bet because of the expectation that they would interrupt their careers for childbirth and rearing during their peak years of productivity. Instead, firms counted on females to stay at home and manage households from which male employees would be largely absent, for the successful worker was expected to be available for work and for after-work socializing until the wee hours. To cope with the economic swings that sometimes brought profits perilously close to the high fixed cost of long-term labor contracts, firms employed core male workers in clerical work on a regular basis and hired females as the part-time buffer force that could be expanded and contracted as necessary. As a result, clerical and service work, though expanding as a percentage of the economy, were never feminized in Japan to the same extent as in the United States.[18]

Germany and Sweden are examples of European coordinated market economies in which labor protections are, unlike Japan, politically mandated and statutorily required. In one sense, the wage compression and protection from dismissal characteristic of European welfare states have a beneficial effect on working women, insofar as females tend to cluster at the lower end of the wage distribution. The median female wage is at about the thirtieth percentile of male wages in both the United States and in Sweden, but the difference in take-home pay between men and women in Sweden is considerably smaller in absolute terms because of the narrower wage spread.[19] As we and others have noted, however, the inadvertent but demonstrable effect of discouraging female employment swamps the salutary effects on wages. Unless there is demand for female labor in compressed wage systems, there will be fewer females to take advantage of the higher wages at the lower end.

The comparison between Sweden and Germany bears out the crucial role of the Swedish public sector in compensating for the private sector's anemic demand for female labor. Under successive left-labor coalitions, the Swedish government expanded public sector employment steadily from the 1970s, accounting for much of the growth in female workforce presence.

This is one of the most notable accomplishments of the political left in Sweden. Although the social democracy traditionally had its stronghold in the mostly male industrial working class, it was able to expand the coalition to include women entering the labor force in large numbers in the 1960s.[20] The coalition was built on a continued commitment to high employment protection and compressed wages and on a simultaneous willingness to expand public services in the face of sluggish private provision. Right parties objected to the pervasive impact of unions on the labor market, but they could not break the power of the unions and were reluctant to expand the size of the service state instead. This in effect meant that the right had no credible alternative to the Social Democrats, and it suffered at the polls as a consequence.

Germany, by contrast, was constrained by ideologically alternating coalitions in government and by an independent central bank to keep its public sector small, at least by Scandinavian standards. The commitment of Christian democracy to a traditionalist view on women and the family, coupled with its historical capacity to attract a sizable share of the industrial working class by endorsing the social market economy (high job and social protection), meant that it was very difficult to built a majority coalition behind a rapid expansion of public services. In retrospect, perhaps the Social Democrats could have drawn the support of a large number of women by aggressively pushing such policies, but they were too concerned with holding on to their blue-collar supporters, who had a credible exit option in the Christian Democratic Union (CDU), and they were obsessed with proving their fiscal "responsibility" to the Bundesbank as well as to the pivotal liberal Center Party, which was passionately committed to market solutions and simultaneously the king-maker in coalitional politics.

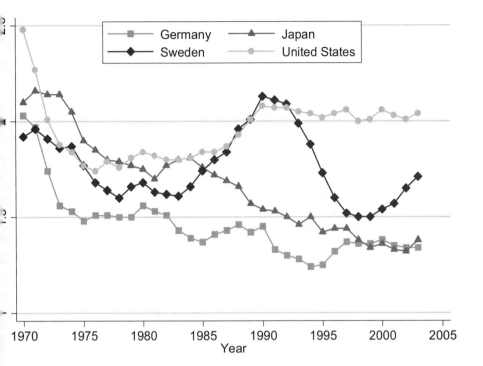

Figure 4.7. Fertility rates in Germany, Japan, Sweden, and the United States, 1970–2005

With less of its economy socialized and a larger percentage of its public sector employees as career bureaucrats than as service providers, Germany has not drawn women into the workforce through government expansion.

The consequences for fertility became visible by the 1980s as demand for female labor in Sweden outstripped that in Germany (see figure 4.7). While fertility in Germany continued its downward slide, Swedish women proved more willing than their German counterparts to have children (although with a notable dip following the recession in the early 1990s). The reason, we suggest, is that Swedish women were less worried about the effects of child-care leave on their careers. If employers do not bear a cost for their employees' discontinuous careers, they do not need to pass along the penalty to their employees.

If career interruption comes at an economic cost, women with high in-

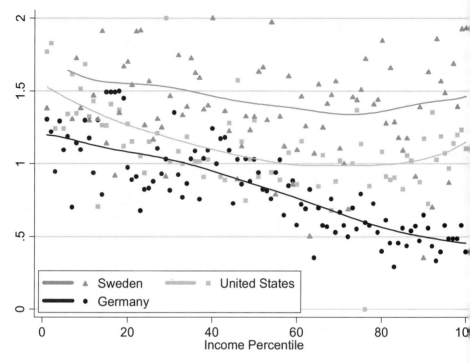

Figure 4.8. Fertility rates of working women in Sweden (top line), the United States (middle line), and Germany (bottom line), by income.

comes ought to have fewer children, and women with fewer children ought to have higher incomes. Figure 4.8 captures the "mommy penalty" in the United States, Germany, and Sweden.[21] As we would expect, the tendency for higher income earning women to have fewer children is more pronounced in Germany than in the United States or in Sweden. The data here understate the difference, for there are fewer German women in managerial positions than in the United States or in Sweden (if we include public sector management) in the first place.

Conclusions

Among rich democracies, fertility is higher where it is easier for women to balance family and career. But the political economy of fertility is not simply a matter of government subsidies to families. It is about the structure of labor markets and production systems, and the effect that public policies can have on these. Labor markets may be women-friendly in an inadvertent way, as in liberal market economies, where the absence of labor market protections reduces the premium attached to career continuity that only men can credibly promise. By unhinging the risk of career discontinuity from quitting a job for the sake of children and home, liberal market economies give females a chance to compete more fairly with men. The United States is a relatively high fertility country despite paltry government spending on child care because the fluid labor market weakens employers' incentives to discriminate against women, allowing many women to balance family and career without Herculean effort. There are, of course, two sides to the liberal market economy solution to gender equality, for the intragender wage disparity that permits career women to outsource much "family work" to low-wage women leaves 25 percent of American children in poverty and substandard child care.

Germany, Japan, and Sweden are all examples of coordinated market economies in which long-term labor contracts and specific skills investment discourage employment of women in the private sector. Although German labor unions are vastly stronger than Japan's, Germany shares with Japan the distinction of being at the bottom of the world's league tables in fertility because the center-left coalitions in Germany have neither expanded the public sector sufficiently to make up for the private sector's anemic demand for female labor, nor has the German government undertaken to bribe firms to hire women who might be more costly human capital investments in the long run. But labor markets may be women-friendly in a deliberate, policy-enhanced way, as in Scandinavia. Private sector employers in Scandinavia may be as loath to hire and to promote women as employers in other coordinated market economies, as evidenced by the striking segmentation of women in public sector jobs. The Scandinavian difference is that governments are sufficiently large to absorb a large proportion of the female working population. Fertility in Scandinavia, as exemplified by the Swedish case in our study, is buoyed by substantial employment of women in the public sector.

The "Dutch Model," which increases access to part-time employment, is sometimes raised as another, more market friendly, way to help women balance the challenges of family and work. The Act on Adjustment of Working Hours passed by the Dutch in 2000 gives employees the right to shorten or increase work hours on request if they have been employed for at least one year.[22] Unlike the postwar Japanese model, in which part-time jobs were low paying and insecure, under the Dutch Model employers in principle pay part-time workers at an hourly wage similar to full-time workers, provide full benefits on a prorated basis, and give workers significant discretion over their work hours.[23] Part-time work is not relegated to low-skill segments of the economy, and it has become widespread in such professions as law and medicine.

The Dutch Model was not, of course, designed to help women. It can be traced to the "Accord of Wassenaar" of November 1982 when employers and unions in the coastal town of Wassenaar sought to end years of fraught industrial relations by signing an agreement to restrain wages in exchange for working time reduction.[24] This flexible labor arrangement became more widespread and part-time jobs grew substantially in the Netherlands during the 1980s and 1990s as employers sought to wriggle out from an entrenched system of job security that is typical of coordinated market economies.

The Dutch case raises two important and related questions. One is whether it is possible to expand part-time employment without undermining the livelihood of Dutch workers generally. In fact, regulation of part-time and temporary employment has been liberalized in many European countries, with the sole exception of France. Unions fear, however, that the move to flexible work could generate a majority coalition in favor of wholesale deregulation, with the result that wage and income inequality could grow rapidly along the model of liberal market economies.[25]

The second question, more central to our current theme, is how part-time employment would affect the plight of women in particular. Flexible work contracts may be at least a partial policy substitute for the expansion of public sector employment boosting demand for female labor, but it also comes with the potential cost of a dual labor market with women in inferior jobs. Unless production technologies and processes change sufficiently to reduce the advantages of specific skills, or unless social mores change such that men are as likely as females to reduce their work hours, part-time employment could become a proxy for the low-wage, general skills "mommy track."

Denmark may be a case that illustrates both the limits and possibilities of reducing employment protection. Job projection has always been relatively low because of the many small firms that have resisted long-term labor contracts, but the government has made up for the shortfall from the private sector by providing generous unemployment benefits and other protection. Denmark's "flexicurity" system is now held up as another "model," but in fact, jobs for women are still primarily in the public sector. To change the sexual division of labor at home so that women are no more burdened than their male counterparts with family work seems both reasonable but still far away.

In a world suffering from environmental degradation, overcrowding, and xenophobia, it may seem perverse to muse about fertility in rich democracies. Our concern is not to provide a template for governments seeking to avoid future workforce shortages by increasing native population growth without resorting to immigration. Rather, our interest in fertility is solely as a barometer of female constraint and opportunity. When the day comes that women can take for granted the possibilities of balancing family and career in a way that men currently do, fertility will become a social and fiscal issue rather than a measure of gender inequality.

Appendix A: Regression Results

The regression results reported in table 4.1 are used to generate figures 4.5 and 4.6. All models in the table are estimated using multilevel, maximum likelihood regression with countries as clusters and assuming normally distributed errors. Model (1) and (2) include a full set of country dummies (not shown), and model (3) and (4) exclude country dummies. The reference groups for the dummy variables are: (1) private sector for the public sector dummy, (2) low education for the educational dummies, and (3) senior managers for the occupational dummies. The reported adjusted R-squared is based on OLS regression.

Table 4.2 shows the macrolevel regressions discussed in the text. Both models are estimated using Prais-Winsten regression with correction for first-order serial correlation and panel corrected standard errors. Both models include a full set of time dummies, but only model (2) includes country fixed effects (and excludes the skill variable as a consequence). The sample consists of thirty-one annual observations for twenty OECD countries (panels). The fertility data are from the Luxembourg Income Study (Luxembourg Employment Study data portions) and the economic data from Penn World Tables (PWT), Mark 6.2 (except for the skill variable, which is described in the text).

Table 4.1. Political economy determinants of fertility among men and women, aged 18–45

	Microlevel results		Multilevel results	
	(1) Women	(2) Men	(3) Women	(4) Men
Age	0.20***	0.02	0.20**	0.02
	(0.05)	(0.04)	(0.05)	(0.04)
Age squared	−0.0029***	−0.0002	−0.0029***	−0.00002
	(0.0007)	(0.0005)	(0.0008)	(0.00005)
Single	−0.74***	−1.01***	−0.74***	−0.99***
	(0.05)	(0.03)	(0.05)	(0.03)
Medium education	−0.09*	−0.11*	−0.04*	−0.13***
	(0.05)	(0.05)	(0.02)	(0.03)
High education	−0.20	−0.13	−0.13*	−0.17***
	(0.12)	(0.10)	(0.07)	(0.05)
Public sector (PS)	0.07***	−0.02*	−0.06*	−0.08
	(0.02)	(0.01)	(0.03)	(0.04)
Govt. consumption (GC)	—	—	−0.03	−0.17***
			(0.07)	(0.04)
PS × GC	—	—	0.28***	0.15**
			(0.06)	(0.07)
Specific skills system	—	—	−0.16**	0.09
			(0.06)	(0.06)
Occupations:				
Professionals	0.15***	−0.03*	0.14***	−0.03
	(0.03)	(0.02)	(0.03)	(0.02)
Associate professionals	0.13***	−0.08***	0.13***	−0.06***
	(0.04)	(0.02)	(0.04)	(0.01)
Clerks	0.11**	−0.08***	0.12***	−0.07***
	(0.04)	(0.02)	(0.04)	(0.02)
Service workers	0.29***	0.02	0.30***	0.02
	(0.09)	(0.04)	(0.08)	(0.03)
Agricultural workers	0.24**	0.07*	0.22**	0.06*
	(0.09)	(0.03)	(0.08)	(0.03)
Craft workers	0.16**	0.02	0.18***	0.02
	(0.05)	(0.03)	(0.04)	(0.02)
Machine operators	0.17***	0.01	0.19***	0.02
	(0.03)	(0.03)	(0.03)	(0.02)
Elementary occupations	0.33***	0.03	0.34***	0.04
	(0.08)	(0.03)	(0.07)	(0.02)
Adj. R-squared	.20	.25	.20	.25
N	92192	107455	92223	109912

Source: OECD, *Factbook 2006.*
Key: ***Significant at a .01 level; **significant at a .05 level; *significant at a .10 level (two-tailed test)

Table 4.2. Political economy determinants of fertility for twenty
OECD countries, 1970–2000

	(1)	(2)
Govt. consumption (GC)	−0.175 (0.164)	−0.006 (0.182)
Specific skills system	−1.206*** (0.202)	—
GC × specific skills system	0.930** (0.375)	0.688* (0.421)
Female labor force participation	−0.005*** (0.002)	−0.003* (0.002)
Average female labor force participation in other countries (lagged one year)	−0.055*** (0.009)	−0.079*** (0.008)
Time fixed effects	Yes	Yes
Country fixed effects	No	Yes
Adj. R-squared	0.869	0.911
N	614	614

Source: OECD, *Factbook 2006.*

Note: Country and time fixed effects not shown.

Key: ***p < .01; **p < .05; *p < .10 (two-tailed test)

5

POLITICAL PREFERENCES

Economic modes of production, by increasing or reducing the premium on a household sexual division of labor, have powerfully circumscribed women's choices in historic time. In the highly interventionist politics of the modern world, however, an exclusive focus on economic structures is likely to miss a big part of the story. Government policies—particularly those that influence the demand for female labor—also have an enormous effect on women's lives.

The possibility of a gender gap in political preferences emerges when marriage contracting is incomplete and termination of the contract is an ever-present possibility. In this case spouses will have conflicting preferences over who receives family benefits, and they will differ over any policies that affect their outside options. This is so not merely, or even primarily, because they could be forced one day to take the outside option but also, as we have argued, because outside options affect the current bargaining power inside the family. Not only does such bargaining power help determine who will have more influence over everyday family decisions, but it also affects the division of household labor (chapter 3) and gender norms (chapter 2).

Government policies may have countervailing effects on women's work opportunities, and some are surely inadvertent. Government policies that protect industrial jobs can, as a side effect, depress labor market opportunities for women because incumbent labor tends to be disproportionately male. Yet government spending on child care and elderly care and public sector service jobs can offset the weak private sector demand for female labor. As long as the job-enhancing effects of government intervention predominate—though this is not always the case—women who work outside the home, or who want insurance against the consequences of divorce, should vote to the left of working men because they value the government spending that makes their jobs possible. At-home women may not necessarily do so because public policies that facilitate female independence do so in part by taxing males who are the breadwinners in more traditional families. In this case the Becker common preference model applies (in effect as a borderline case of the general bargaining model).

We have also argued that demand for female labor undermines patriarchal norms, freeing women to be more equal participants in many aspects of life. If women recognize that patriarchal values bind them with invisible ribbons, as it were, they should favor government policies that increase the demand for female labor and, by extension, release women from unquestioned servitude.[1] As we argued in chapter 2, the causal logic also moves in the opposite direction, reinforcing norm change. Parents who seek to strengthen the position of their daughters in the labor market will be inclined to teach their sons and daughters gender equality at home and will be predisposed to favor educational policies that incorporate such equality into the public school curriculum.

As we have argued, women are generally at a disadvantage when competing for jobs with men because they are expected to leave the labor market for purposes of childbirth and rearing.[2] Employers will therefore be reluctant to invest in skills of women, and young women are likewise hesitant to build up substantial employer-specific assets or even invest in the education that is needed for a specific skills type of job since these may be forfeited with the birth of their first child.[3]

How great the motherhood disadvantage is, however, depends on the nature of skills that employers are seeking.[4] If such skills are highly specific to firms, or even to industries, and if a substantial part of training is paid by the employer, there is a strong disincentive to make these investments in female employees where the average time horizon is comparatively short. This is reinforced by women's own decisions because they are disinclined to invest in specific skills for which they are at a disadvantage. Women are therefore more likely than men to invest in general skills and/or in skills that are less prone to deteriorate when not used for some period of time. If women choose to invest in skills, they should choose skill sets that are perennially in demand and that can be updated relatively easily following labor market absences. It is the emergence of these types of jobs in services that have made it possible for women to specialize in marketable, as opposed to household-specific, skills. Yet their relative abundance varies systematically according to the type of production regime or variety of capitalism—a logic that is simply a specific application of our general mode of production argument.

Females sort themselves into different kinds of jobs from males to avoid taking a hit in pay or promotion prospects with employers who value work continuity and learning on the job. Women have a comparative *dis*advantage in specific labor market skills just as they have a comparative disadvantage in hard manual labor. Economies that place a premium on specific skills therefore put women at a disadvantage compared to economies that emphasize general skills, in which women are at an equal footing with men if we assume that labor is not physically highly challenging and that women do not have a strong absolute advantage in household skills.

Countries differ in the degree to which their labor markets utilize specific skills. For a variety of reasons, some countries have specialized in forms of production that use specific skills intensely, whereas employers in other countries invest minimally in their workers for a more fluid labor force.[5] These differences in production strategies are reinforced by institutions that accompany them, in particular strong unions and centralized collective bargaining institutions. Unions protect workers with specific skills, in part through public policies such as employment protection legislation, and centralized bargaining suppresses the supply of service sector jobs at the lower end of the productivity and wage distribution. Our argument implies that women in more flexible labor markets are typically better able to compete on an equal footing with men in the labor market because investments in skills are mostly borne by workers rather than by employers—say, through college education—and because general skills do not depend on staying with a particular employer for a long period of time. This implies that, everything else being equal, female labor market participation tends to be lower in specific skills systems.[6]

As we argued in chapter 3, however, these effects can be mediated by social and economic policies deliberately designed to counter them. In particular, the government can compensate for the exclusion of women from good jobs in the private sector by supporting women's ability to form an independent household, especially through publicly provided services such as day care.[7] The Scandinavian countries are prime examples here, having attained high female participation rates by creating a large, and heavily feminized, public sector.[8] This, then, implies a role for democratic politics in affecting the bargaining power between the sexes, and this in turn suggests that policy preferences between the sexes should diverge. Universal suffrage turns gender politics into a potential independent variable in explaining power between the sexes.[9] As a result, the conflict of interest within the household can also be manifested in the form of a gender gap in partisan preferences.

The "Old" Gender Gap

Women's move to the left in rich democracies is striking because women typically voted to the right of men in these countries only a few decades ago.[10] In countries where the demand for female labor is limited —or for women with limited economic opportunities in any country— women are *more* likely than men to be socially conservative despite the unflattering roles their conservatism gives them to play. As we suggested in chapter 2, the reason is that women for whom the marriage market is the principal way to secure a livelihood seek to shore up the sanctity and strength of family values. Once committed to the life of a married woman, that marriage is best that binds securely and for which obligations are taken seriously by the man as well as by the woman.[11] An interesting example of this is Islamic fundamentalism, which places serious restrictions on female behavior but also commits husbands to take care of their wives. In Islamic countries with limited demand for female labor, women are more likely than their male counterparts to hold fundamentalist views. Families are presumably careful to socialize their daughters to hold traditional beliefs when their daughters have only the marriage market to rely on for their livelihoods. Once married, a woman is better off with a devout husband than one who does not take seriously his religious obligations to family.

The New Gender Gap

Starting in the late 1960s in the United States and Scandinavia, and for some years thereafter in many other Western countries, women began moving out of sync with their husbands in their voting behavior, often voting to the left of men in aggregate.[12] Women are more likely than their male counterparts to support activist government across a range of economic policies.[13]

In economic efficiency models of the family there is no room for men and women to favor different public policies. *Families* will differ over social policies depending on their position in the age and class structure and the like, but individual family members will favor policies that maximize the welfare of the household, and these are the ones that enable a complete division of labor and maximize the income of the male breadwinner. Men and women are therefore assumed to have more or less identical preferences.

There are several competing explanations for "the modern gender gap," where women's preferences and voting patterns appear to be moving to the left. Some scholars argue that women are more altruistic than men and that they therefore favor more welfare spending.[14] But this argument is a static one that fails to explain the change in voting behavior over recent decades. Other scholars have pointed out that women are more likely than men to be economically vulnerable.[15] But survey research suggests that women throughout the wage distribution are more likely to vote left than their male counterparts.[16] Class status is not capturing the whole story, although this account implicitly assumes—correctly we believe—that the aggregate welfare of the household is not all that matters.

One way to move beyond the notion that gender conflict is simply an expression of class conflict is to consider that high divorce rates leave all women at a higher risk of income loss than before, and that women are therefore voting for more redistribution even before they receive it, as a form of insurance.[17] Using variation in divorce rates across U.S. states and some European countries, Edlund and Pande derive a measure of "divorce risk" and find that it corresponds with the likelihood of women voting further left than their socioeconomic status warrants.

If women vote left as insurance against post-divorce poverty, we would expect that women staying out of the workforce are at the greatest risk and hence most likely to vote left. Instead, however, the data suggest that women in the workforce are more likely to vote left than housewives.[18] This suggests that the insurance argument is missing something important, since working women have already reduced their economic exposure to the possibility of divorce.[19]

The data suggest to us an alternative, or at least complementary, explanation based on household bargaining: working women gain bargaining power at home from the partial socialization of family work, such as child care and elderly care, and these are precisely the sorts of policies that parties on the left are more likely to espouse. The logic is that with some of her family burden lifted by the public purse, a woman is better able to invest in her marketable skills. By raising her level of economic independence closer to her husband's, a wife reduces her stake in keeping the relationship going closer to his level. As we argued in chapter 3, we should observe more equal shares of family work in the household not only because the government is undertaking part of it but also because a woman is less willing to give up increasing amounts of her time to keep the marriage from dissolving.

But there are reasons for women in traditional marriages not to be swayed by the bargaining logic and vote with their husbands rather than their working sisters. If a woman has invested heavily in household-specific skills her opportunities in the labor markets are correspondingly low, and her material welfare will be tied up with the job security and income of the male breadwinner. Policies that favor the male breadwinner are therefore also policies that benefit women who are more or less completely dependent on their husbands. This is where the Becker model is useful. Precisely because the division of labor is more or less complete in traditional households, they can in effect be treated as unitary actors with a single utility function (as Becker does).

Consequently when a woman has sunk all her investments into household-specific skills, paid employment options will always be relatively unattractive, and so are costly policies to pay for day care and public employment. If divorce cannot be ruled out, insurance policies for these women will tend to focus on the responsibilities of ex-husbands—especially alimony and child support. It is when women make serious investments in marketable skills that the division of household labor itself becomes contested, and this is true as well of public policies that affect this division. There is thus a "tipping point" beyond which it makes sense for women to support public policies that improve opportunities to engage in paid employment, even if this undermines the income and protection of core, skilled, male workers to whom they may be married. The lower the investment in household-specific skills, the more reason women have for favoring public policies that diverge from men's preferences.

As we suggested in chapter 2, the logic can be more formally represented as a network or strategic complementarities game, which is illustrated in figure 5.1. The idea is that the decision of any women to enter the labor market (captured as a probability on the y-axis) has consequences for the probability of other women doing the same. These strategic complementarities arise because (1) women who enter the labor market will demand and supply services that incentivize other women to enter; (2) increased female labor force participation reduces the gains from the gender division of labor and increases divorce rates, which in turn increases the incentives of women to become financially independent; and (3) socialization patterns change to make women more likely to want active careers. In steady state these probabilities must be the same for otherwise similar individuals, and this happens in figure 5.1 when the individual response function to female labor force participation intersects the 45-degree line. The nature of equilibria depends on the composition of demand for skills, which is in turn a function of service sector employment and the production system.

In figure 5.1. we capture the common effects of deindustrialization as an upward shift of the S curve, and the differences in outcomes across political economies as the two stable equilibria, L′ and H′. Following the analysis in chapter 3, countries that specialize in production that requires intensive use of specific skills disfavor female participation in the economy and have notable lower female labor force participation and divorce rates than others. In the L equilibrium women tend to be dependent on a male breadwinner, and only the minority who are unmarried and working full time are likely to have preferences for public policies that diverge sharply from those of males. The distribution of preferences is the opposite in the H equilibrium, associated with general skills countries or countries with a large public sector, where most women will work, or want to

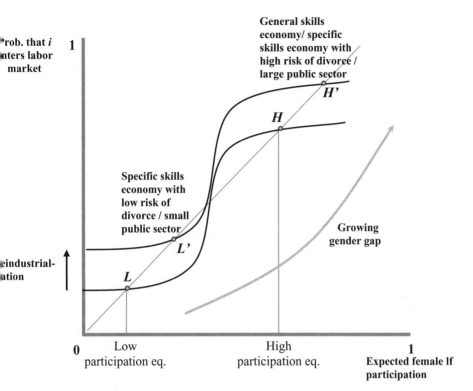

Figure 5.1. Multiple equilibria in the female labor market entry game

work, and favor policies that improve their outside options. The traditional family will be defended by only a small minority. As we move from low to high equilibria, we thus expect the gender gap in preferences to rise.

The welfare state matters to the story because it is an important source of employment for women and replaces so many of the caring functions that are otherwise provided "for free" in the family. The importance of public employment is particularly salient in specific skills countries where it can compensate for reduced opportunities for women in the private labor market. A large public sector may therefore push specific skill countries into the high equilibrium outcome in figure 5.1. Public employment is consequently also a matter of potential gender conflict.

The most obvious matter of preference divergence between men and women, perhaps, is publicly subsidized day care. Since women are much more likely to end up as primary caregivers, their welfare is disproportionately affected by the availability of high-quality, low-cost day care. Men may prefer to spare the public purse and hence their tax bill if their wives are default child care givers. The same is true for women who depend heavily on a male breadwinner, which, again, is more likely in some countries rather than others. This logic also applies to public care for the elderly and the sick because it helps women escape some of their traditional duties and thereby permits more time in paid employment.

Support for redistribution and social insurance obviously does not come from women alone. Any person with an income below the mean is likely to prefer at least some redistributive spending. And when an insurance motive is added to the model, those exposed to greater risks will also demand more spending. One key source of such risks is the transferability of workers' skills. The harder it is to transport skills from one job to another, the greater the importance of income protection though social insurance programs (guaranteed health care, pensions, unemployment benefits, job security, and so on).

The key implications of our argument are that women at any given level of income and skill specificity will prefer higher social protection than men, but that the magnitude of the difference depends on the national skill system and the size of the public sector. The gender gap will be magnified by an indirect effect through income insofar as women earn less than men. On the other hand, the effect is reduced to the extent that women invest more in general than in specific skills. An interesting corollary of this argument is that women should be more supportive than men of public investment in general education. Inexpensive access to good formal education presumably benefits women disproportionately because they have a comparative advantage in general skills.

Empirical Analysis: Data and Measurement

To test our hypotheses we first turn to the 1996 International Social Survey Programme (ISSP) on the role of government. These data contain a number of questions about government spending and social policy as well as information on the key independent variables. We have complete data for ten advanced democracies (Australia, Britain, Canada, France, Germany, Ireland, Norway, New Zealand, Sweden, and United States). Subsequently we will also discuss some evidence on gender norms from the 1994 ISSP survey on the family used in chapter 3.

Unfortunately the 1996 survey does not ask questions that speak directly to policies that differentially affect men and women. There are no questions, for example, about spending on child care or care for the elderly, and many of the other spending questions—about pensions, unemployment, and so on—are not clearly related to gender conflict. Three questions, however, address the role of the government in providing job opportunities, and we have argued that this is an important determinant of women's employment opportunities outside the family as well as of their bargaining power within it. It ought to be a matter of gender conflict. The three questions ask whether the government should (1) finance projects to create new jobs, (2) reduce the working week to produce more jobs, and (3) be responsible for providing jobs for all who want to work. Respondents could express different levels of support or opposition, and we combined the answers into a single public employment support index, which ranges from 1 (strong opposition) to 5 (strong support).

The second dependent variable is declared affiliation or support for a left or center-left party.[20] Although this variable does not directly capture differences in policy preferences, left parties tend to be more supportive of policies that would promote gender equality, and the measure has the advantage of being clearly politically salient. If women are indeed seeking a more active role for the government in securing gender equality, it is reasonable to expect that left support will be greater among women (the average support among all respondents is 43 percent). The variable is coded 1 for center-left and 0 for center-right support. Parties classified as left in each country are listed in appendix A.

The gender gap in preferences is modeled simply as the difference in preferences between men and women, estimated by a gender dummy variable (1 = women, 0 = men). To test whether the gender gap varies across groups and countries, we interact this variable with labor force participation, marital status, risk of divorce, and skill system. Labor force participation is measured as in chapter 3 (full-time employed are coded 1, part-time employed 0.5, less than part-time employed 0.25, and those who consider themselves homemakers or who are retired are coded 0). The skill system is again measured as a function of firm tenure rates and vocational training activity. Unlike the 1994 data used in chapter 3, however, there is no variable that allows us to gauge the risk, or perceived risk, of divorce at the level of the individual. Instead we use national divorce rates, defined as the percentage of marriages ending in divorce.[21] In 1996 these rates varied from 10 in Ireland to 67 in Sweden. Because it eases the interpretation of the results, the variable is standardized to vary between 0 and 1. In addition, we distinguish between those who are married and those who are not. One might sensibly expect that unmarried people demand more social protection because they are unable to pool risks within the family. But this should be particularly true of women who tend to be in more vulnerable labor market positions. One can loosely think of being unmarried as a realized risk of having to rely on outside options.

In addition we control for several of the variables used in chapter 3: age, education, retirement, religiosity, Catholicism, and income (defined the same way). We also add a variable for unemployment, as well as one for the skill specificity of individuals. As explained above, women have less of an incentive than men to invest in specific skills, and such skills tend to increase the demand for social protection. We therefore need to compare men and women with similar skill sets. The variable is based on information on the general education and occupation of the respondent.[22]

Empirical Estimation and Results

The starting point is the same general multilevel model outlined in the appendix to chapter 3. We begin at the individual level and examine how the gender gap varies across those who are in and outside of the labor market, and those who are married and those who are not. Figure 5.2 illustrates the substantive results for public employment and left partisanship (the detailed results are reported in columns [1] and [2] of table 5.2 in appendix B, and in columns [5] and [6] for left partisanship).[23] In interpreting these it is important to note that all regressions use country-specific intercepts so that every contextually specific factor that may affect changes in policy away from the status quo have been

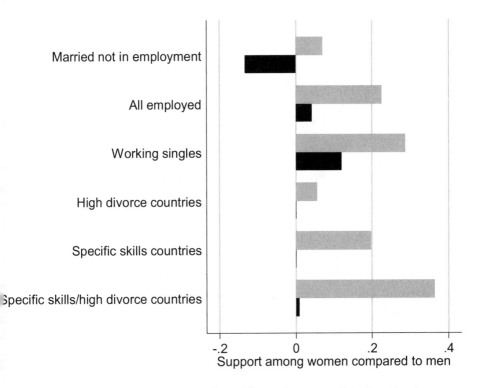

Figure 5.2. The gender gap in support for public employment policies (gray bars) and the political left (black bars)
Note: Predicted gaps are based on the multilevel regression results reported in table 5.2 in appendix B. The gap in support for public employment policies is measured as standard deviations on the dependent variable. The gap in support for the left is measured as the probability of women voting left minus the probability of men voting left.

controlled for. What interests us here is the gender gap in preferences for change—including differences in that gap across countries. We are *not* trying to explain cross-national difference in the overall level of support for change.

Comparing the gap for different subgroups it is evident that there exists only a statistically significant net gender gap in preferences for public jobs provision, not for left party support. The gap in support for public employment policies is quite large, however, with women in all cases being considerably more supportive. The net difference across all groups is equivalent to about 21 percent of a standard deviation on the dependent variable. Unfortunately, it is very hard to give substantive meaning to this number because we do not know how any particular level of agreement with any of the questions maps onto actual (changes in) budgetary commitments. We do know, however, that gender is one of the best predictors of preferences as measured by support for public employment policies, and there is a statistically significant gender gap on this variable in each one of our ten countries.[24] Insofar as there are politically meaningful differences in voter policy preferences—and we have every reason to expect that there are—gender is therefore a key variable in explaining these.

The same is not true of support for the left, where gender differences in the sample as a whole are small. In part, at least, this is because parties offer packages of policies that do not clearly map onto interest conflicts between men and women—we return to this issue below—but it is also in part because the net number disguises notable differences across subgroups of respondents. Thus, among those who participate in the labor market, women are considerably more likely than men to support expansive employment policies and left parties. The same is the case for singles (or more precisely "unmarried" since some will likely be in relationships). In fact, married women outside the labor market (represented by the top two bars) are only marginally more likely than men to support public employment, and they are in fact about 13 percent *less* likely than men to support left and center-left parties. After controlling for age, income, and so on, married housewives are thus quite conservative—a fact that makes good sense in terms of the theory and helps explain why countries with a traditional family structure and low female labor force participation tend to exhibit small gender gaps. This is the case represented by the low-participation equilibrium in figure 5.1.

The other relationships that emerge from the regressions (not shown in figure 5.2) are the negative effect of income, as predicted by a simple Meltzer-Richard redistribution argument, and the positive effect of individual skill specificity, as predicted by the asset model of social policy preferences. General education, however, does not play any independent role. Skills and income are less salient in explaining support for the left (although the effects are in the right direction and usually significant), whereas religiosity, but not Catholicism, assumes a more important role as a significant negative predictor of support for left parties. The negative relationship between religion and left support jibes well with the predictions of Roemer's multidimensional model of distributive politics.[25] Religion does indeed appear to reduce support for the left.

The other results reported in figure 5.2 (based on models 3–4 and 7–8 in table 5.2) exploit another possibility in multilevel modeling: cross-level interactions.[26] Specifically, we have argued that the gender gap may vary according to the probability of divorce, which varies across countries and can be measured only at that level in our data, and we have also suggested that the gap is likely to be particularly large in specific skills countries when divorce rates are high (since women are more disadvantaged in the private labor market when the emphasis in production on specific skill is high). Whether the effect of specific skill systems is positive or negative after control for divorce is hard to know because we cannot specify the location of the "tipping point" ex ante. This is especially true since there is a feedback effect of demand for a large public sector on female labor force participation, and hence preferences (we will add public sector employment to the analysis below, although it creates obvious problems of endogeneity). For now we simply note that as divorce rates rise, the likelihood that the gap is larger in specific skill economies also rises.

It turns out that the estimated parameters for the cross-level interactions are correctly signed, but in the case of left partisanship they are weak and statistically insignificant. Support for public employment, in contrast, is quite strongly dependent on especially skill specificity, although the parameters are imprecisely estimated—partly a result of muliticollinearity. In the version where the national-level variables are interacted—which best reflects our theoretical argument—the gender gap is significantly different across countries with different combinations of divorce rates and skill systems. Where divorce rates are high and/or skills tend to be specific, the gender gap is larger (see the last two bars in figure 5.2.)

An intriguing question is why the divorce rate is not more important in accounting for the gender gap in partisanship. The fact that women who work or who are not married are significantly more likely to support both the left and public employment clearly suggests that concern for outside options is important. But it appears that the political right is quite successful in attracting the support of some women by advocating "family values" that may be seen as a way to reduce divorce and enhance women's security within the traditional family. Our data cannot help us sort this out, but it is an issue that future research should address.

Figure 5.3 provides a graphical summary of the range of estimated results for different subgroups in different national systems. For each of four different combinations of marital status, labor market participation, divorce rates, and skill system the figure shows the gender gap in support for public employment policies and left parties. As before, the gap is measured in standard deviations on the dependent public employment variable and as the probability of supporting a left or center-left party. We see that married women outside paid employment living in a country with low divorce rates, or a general skills economy, may well be more conservative in their political preferences than men. Certainly that is the case in terms of left party support. With labor market participation, however, preferences for a more active government intensify, and unmarried women are also notably more "left-leaning" than men. At least for preferences over employment policies, the gender gap is particularly large in specific skills countries with high divorce rates. Here married women in paid employment are estimated to be nearly one-half a standard deviation more supportive of an active role of the government in employment creation than men, and they are notably more likely to support a left or center-left party than men (13 percent more likely compared to 13 percent *less* likely when women are married, not working, and living in a general skills or low divorce country).

The results are thus broadly consistent with the argument that the gender gap varies across countries according to divorce rates and labor market conditions. In fact the cross-country differences are greater than what is readily apparent in figure 5.3 because labor force participation rates vary across countries, and we know that paid employment makes women more "left-leaning." In 1996 (the year of the survey), for example, female labor force participation was 49 percent in Ireland but 74 percent in Sweden. For 25 percent of women in these countries, therefore, the predicted effect on preferences would be equivalent to the difference between the first and second set of bars in figure 5.2. In terms of the probability of supporting the left among these women, this difference translates into a 16

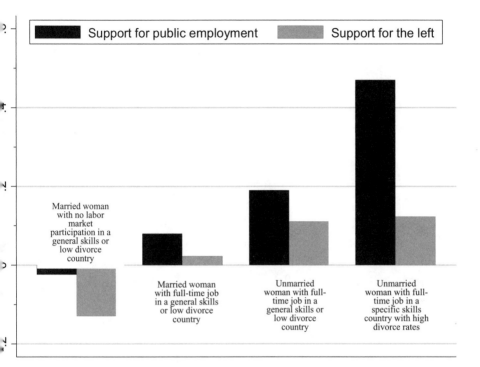

Figure 5.3. The gender gap in support for public employment and left parties
Note: The bars show the predicted difference between men and women in their support for public employment policies and left parties, where a positive gap means greater support among women. The gap in support for public employment is measured in standard deviations of the dependent variable. The gap in support for the left is measured in differences in the probability of voting for a left party.

percent higher probability in Sweden. No wonder the Swedish Social Democrats are reluctant to give in to perceived pressures to cut back on the public provision of welfare services.

Norms and the Two Equilibria

We can extend the analysis to gender norms, which, like public policy preferences, should vary with labor force participation and the other variables we have identified. Norms are captured by two questions in the 1994 survey, which ask respondents to indicate their level of agreement with statements that represent traditional views on gender roles and the family. One reads "a man's job is to earn money; a woman's job is to look after the home and family"; the other "when there are children in the family, parents should stay together even if they don't get along." A factor analysis shows that these items have the highest loadings on an underlying dimension that can reasonably be interpreted as capturing more or less "traditionalist" views on the family and gender roles. We combined the variables in a simple index that varies from 1 (most traditionalist) to 5 (least traditionalist).

Since the dependent variable does not refer to change, these questions can also reasonably be used to tap differences in norms across countries, not just across individuals. We can therefore use the skill system, government consumption, and their interaction as predictors, whereas in the preferences regressions in table 5.1 the effects of these variables are absorbed into the country-specific intercepts. The full regression results are shown in table 5.2 in appendix B. Here we focus exclusively on the relationships between skills, government consumption, and norms (see table 5.1), which allows us to capture the two equilibrium outcomes in figure 5.1 very neatly. Where possible, we compare the results to those for preferences for public employment, which we have estimated on the 1994 data using a similar model (second column in table 5.3 in appendix B).

The two columns for norms in table 5.1 show the estimated values on the norms index for each combination of values on the skill and government consumption variables (using their minimum and maximum). *Level* refers to the absolute support for particular norms in the general population, and the gender gap is the difference between men and women.[27] Each entry is shown in terms of number of standard deviations on the dependent variable (which is roughly equal to the difference between two answer categories, such as "agree" and "neither agree nor disagree"). Positive numbers mean that the average responses in a cell deviate toward less traditionalist (or more gender "egalitarian") views, and negative numbers mean that the average responses deviate toward more traditionalist views. The cell representing general skills and low government consumption is used as the comparison group (and therefore set to 0).

Note that norms in specific skills systems without large public service

Table 5.1. The relationship between skill system, size of public service sector, and gender-equal norms and preferences

			Size of public service sector			
			Small		Large	
			Norms	Preferences	Norms	Preferences
Skill system	General	Level	0	—	0.09	—
		Gender gap	0.51	0.34	0.45	0.18
	Specific	Level	−1.20	—	0.39	—
		Gender gap	−1.36	−0.61	0.92	0.63

Note: Based on multilevel regression results from table 5.3 in appendix B. Entries are measured as proportions of standard deviations on the dependent variable. The cell representing general skills and low government consumption is used as the comparison group (= 0).

sectors deviate strongly in a traditionalist direction compared to the reference cell (the difference is 1.2 standard deviations). By contrast, specific skills countries with large public service sectors exhibit nontraditionalist values, even compared to general skills systems that also have large public sectors. As in the network game presented in figure 5.1, this suggests distinct equilibria where specific skills systems with the least favorable labor market opportunities for women are associated with the most traditionalist values, and general skills systems and specific skills systems with a large, feminized public service sector—both more conducive to women's labor market participation—exhibit more egalitarian gender and family norms. Norms, economic structure, and policies, in other words, are complements.

This conclusion is supported when we look at the gender *gap* in norms as well as in preferences. A positive number here means that women are less traditionalist than men and that they favor a greater role for the government in generating employment. What is immediately apparent when looking at these numbers is that women in specific skills systems with a small public sector are very traditionalist compared to men, at the same time as they are not very favorably disposed toward an expanded role for the state. As argued above, this makes good sense in terms of an equilibrium since if women are heavily dependent on a male breadwinner for their welfare, they may rationally support traditional family values and refrain from supporting policies that will raise taxes on male insiders. By contrast, women are less traditionalist than men in general skills systems and in countries with a large public sector. Having already established a foothold in the labor market, women are thus much less beholden to traditional family and gender roles. And where the public sector (as opposed to the market) is critical in maintaining and improving their outside options, they are strongly in favor of expansionary public employment policies.

The critical insight from this analysis is that public policies can notably affect the economic opportunity structure, and hence halt or accelerate the transition away from patriarchal norms. Because norms, preferences, and policies are complements, once changes get under way they can be sudden and wide-ranging. Gender and family norms were fundamentally reshaped in a few decades in Scandinavia, for example. We suspect that changes of similar proportions are about to erupt in countries in southern Europe and perhaps East Asia—which are thus far holdouts for traditionalist views on women and the family. Our hunch comes from the reversal of the relationship between female labor force participation and fertility that we documented in chapter 4. This relationship has turned positive in recent years, causing a fertility crisis in countries where (paradoxically) most women are still at home. To us, this suggests a growing desire by women to have careers, which runs up against traditionalist family policies that reduce women's opportunities in the labor market. This is a sign of an emerging disequilibrium, which will be resolved only when public policies adapt and improve women's access to paid employment. When that happens, our argument implies, significant changes in norms will follow.

So What?

Our results turn on their heads some claims that are sometimes made about gender and political preferences. Orloff (1993, 1999) and O'Connor, Orloff, and Shaver (1999), for example, strongly suggest that women are most disadvantaged in countries, such as those in southern Europe and East Asia, where female labor force participation rates are low, stratification on the labor market high, and the distribution of domestic work very unequal. If access to paid work and the ability to form autonomous households are fundamental interests of women, as Orloff and others argue, one would expect gender conflicts to be most intense in these countries. Yet, these are countries in which the policy preferences of men and women appear the most *similar* and where there does not appear to be a strong gender gap in electoral politics. An explanation for this puzzle is that the family as an institution is heavily protected through labor market conditions and reinforced by legislation and norms against divorce. The likelihood of a first marriage ending in divorce in Italy is less than one in ten—even lower than the 1950s United States. In addition, female labor force participation rates are very low, which also help to align the interests of men and women.

Another controversy surrounds the role of the public-private sector division in Scandinavia. According to some, this division—which concerns issues of public sector size, relative pay, and public sector job protection—has emerged as a salient cleavage in electoral politics. But as Pierson points out, since men in the private sector tend to be married to women in the public sector, there is no compelling reason that spouses should quibble over issues of relative pay (2000, 807). At the end of the day, the income of both spouses simply adds to family income. But this logic applies only when husband and wife have few reasons to concern themselves with outside options. And since pay in the public sector is financed by taxing the private sector, policies affecting relative pay are a perfect example of an area where gender conflict is likely to be intense.

A third puzzle concerns the persistent and widespread tendency of women to be less likely than men to support global economic integration. In a very careful empirical paper, Burgoon and Hiscox (2004) suggest that the "gender gap" in trade preferences might reflect economic illiteracy of women compared to men, and that the trend toward education equality might, in time, eliminate the gap. Our analysis of the political gender gap, which includes a control for education, invites skepticism about this conclusion. We expect that the gender gap in trade preferences reflects, as we have suggested, a greater likelihood that women are employed in the public sector. Whether or not it is sensible to think that economic integration will hurt public employment, it seems that both men and women tend to think that this is the case, suggesting that the gap is due to differences in policy preferences rather than in macroeconomic theorizing.

Conclusions

If patriarchy can be thought of as female resignation, the gender voting gap reflects a feisty dissatisfaction with the status quo. In rich democracies, working women rely on government services, and in some cases government employment, to maintain their bargaining position in marriage. Because of democracy and universal suffrage, coupled with the rise of state power, gender relations have become politicized. The gender gap in policy preferences suggests that many women are hoping to use the democratic state to make them more egalitarian still.

The availability of policies to promote gender equality bodes well for women in poor countries for whom the wait for the arrival of the service economy seems intolerably long. In Indian village councils, a quota system for female and lower caste representation sets up a natural experiment to see what happens in village councils with female representation, apart from the factors that would have led voters to choose female delegates in the first place. In the Indian case, councils led by women are more likely to reflect female voter preferences, for example, for clean drinking water and passable roads.[28]

That's the good news. Less encouraging is the systematic underrepresentation of women in all democracies, save in a few Scandinavian countries. In the next chapter, we examine the reasons for lagging female political representation, as well as the reasons for its variation across democracies.

Appendix A: Parties Coded as Left or Center-Left

Country	Party
Australia	Greens, Labour
Britain	Labour
Canada	Communists, NDP, Bloc Quebecois, Greens
France	Communists, Socialist Party
Germany	PDS, SPD, Greens
Ireland	Worker's Party, Sinn Fein, Democratic Left
Norway	Labor, Socialist Left
New Zealand	Red Alliance, Labour
Sweden	Alliance, Labor, Socialists
United States	Democrats

Table 5.2. The gender gap in social preferences and left party support

	Public employment					Left partisanship		
	(1)	(2)	(3)	(4)	(5)	(6)	(7)	(8)
Female	0.174***	0.057	−0.031	−0.022	0.154	−0.552**	−0.896*	−0.563*
	(0.032)	(0.041)	(0.115)	(0.050)	(0.133)	(0.222)	(0.467)	(0.304)
Female × labor force participation	—	0.113**	0.115**	0.124**	—	0.729***	0.753***	0.731***
		(0.037)	(0.048)	(0.050)		(0.188)	(0.191)	(0.191)
Female × unmarried	—	0.066**	0.064**	0.062**	—	0.315**	0.312**	0.314**
		(0.029)	(0.029)	(0.030)		(0.111)	(0.112)	(0.113)
Female × divorce	—	—	0.046	—	—	—	0.007	—
			(0.14)				(0.006)	
Female × skill specificity	—	—	0.162	—	—	—	0.006	—
			(0.125)				(0.373)	
Female × divorce × skill specificity	—	—	—	0.298**	—	—	—	0.038
				(0.117)				(0.482)
Labor force participation	0.077	−0.017	−0.032	−0.041	0.514**	−0.049	−0.071	−0.052
	(0.045)	(0.044)	(0.048)	(0.050)	(0.214)	(0.292)	(0.303)	(0.296)
Unmarried	0.057***	0.024	0.025	0.026	0.175*	0.011	0.013	0.011
	(0.016)	(0.023)	(0.023)	(0.023)	(0.091)	(0.106)	(0.104)	(0.103)

(continued)

Table 5.2. Continued

	Public employment				Left partisanship			
	(1)	(2)	(3)	(4)	(5)	(6)	(7)	(8)
Income (log)	-0.003***	-0.003***	-0.003***	-0.003***	-0.003	-0.003*	-0.003*	-0.003*
	(0.001)	(0.0005)	(0.0005)	(0.0005)	(0.002)	(0.002)	(0.002)	(0.002)
Individual skill specificity	0.100***	0.100***	0.099***	0.098***	0.240**	0.246**	0.242**	0.246**
	(0.023)	(0.023)	(0.022)	(0.023)	(0.083)	(0.084)	(0.084)	(0.083)
Age	-0.001	-0.001	-0.001	-0.001	0.002	0.001	0.001	0.001
	(0.002)	(0.001)	(0.001)	(0.001)	(0.005)	(0.006)	(0.006)	(0.006)
Education	-0.013	-0.013	-0.015	-0.015	0.080	0.079	0.078	0.078
	(0.020)	(0.020)	(0.020)	(0.020)	(0.081)	(0.080)	(0.080)	(0.080)
Retirement	0.066	0.018	0.005	0.0002	0.120	-0.149	-0.164	-0.150
	(0.056)	(0.052)	(0.061)	(0.061)	(0.288)	(0.309)	(0.305)	(0.302)
Unemployment	0.197**	0.156*	0.141*	0.135	0.628	0.427	0.417	0.425
	(0.081)	(0.086)	(0.061)	(0.082)	(0.420)	(0.410)	(0.411)	(0.410)
Religiosity	-0.012	-0.012	-0.011	-0.011	-0.121*	-0.122*	-0.122**	-0.122**
	(0.009)	(0.009)	(0.009)	(0.008)	(0.051)	(0.050)	(0.049)	(0.049)
Catholic	-0.019	-0.016	-0.017	-0.017	-0.261	-0.252	-0.257	-0.253
	(0.105)	(0.104)	(0.105)	(0.104)	(0.293)	(0.293)	(0.295)	(0.293)
No. of countries	10	10	10	10	10	10	10	10
N	7460	7460	7460	7460	5793	5793	5793	5793

Note: The entries are maximum likelihood estimates with estimated standard errors in parentheses. Left partisanship was estimated using binominal logistic regression. All models have country-specific intercepts (not shown).

Key: ***p < .01; **p < .05; *p < .10

Table 5.3. Determinants of norms and preferences compared

	Norms (nontraditional/"liberal")	Preferences (more public employment)
Number of dependents	−0.04*** (0.01)	−0.00 (0.01)
Age	−0.02** (0.001)	−0.003* (0.001)
Education	0.14*** (0.02)	−0.10*** (0.02)
Religiosity	−0.10*** (0.01)	−0.02** (0.01)
Catholic	0.17** (0.05)	0.03 (0.07)
Female	0.52*** (0.05)	0.25** (0.08)
Skill specificity	−1.03** (0.36)	—
Public sector	0.27 (0.39)	—
Public sector × skill specificity	1.13 (0.79)	—
Female × skill specificity	−0.36** (0.12)	−0.44** (0.18)
Female × public sector	−0.33** (0.11)	−0.10 (0.26)
Female × public sector × skill specificity	0.74** (0.21)	0.80 (0.46)
N	12460	10227
No. of countries	12	11

Note: The entries are maximum likelihood estimates with estimated standard errors in parentheses. The model for preferences uses country-specific intercepts (not shown).

Key: ***p < .01; **p < .05; *p < .10

6

GENDER AND POLITICAL CAREERS: A COMPARATIVE LABOR MARKET ANALYSIS OF FEMALE POLITICAL REPRESENTATION

Females are strikingly underrepresented in the world's legislatures, though the variation among rich democracies is enormous, ranging from 9 percent in Japan and 14 percent in the United States at the low end to parity in Sweden at the high end. These examples are illustrative of a pattern, for the prevailing wisdom is correct that proportional representation (PR) systems are friendlier to successful female candidacy than district systems. Indeed, in Japan, 6.3 percent of the parliamentarians elected from single-member districts are females, compared to 13.3 percent elected from party lists on proportional representation ballots. Although 13.3 percent is still low by world standards, it is double the district line-up returned by the same voters in the same election, and the current electoral system has been in place only since 1994. Clearly, cultural preferences leave substantial variation unexplained.

Exactly how proportional representation rules help the cause of female candidates, however, is only dimly understood. In this chapter we apply the embedded bargaining framework to explain how electoral rules and other factors shape the labor markets in political careers across countries and systematically help or hurt women considering their role as primary caregivers in the family. Markets for professional politicians, we argue, function in a manner that is not very different from markets in other professions, except that political institutions (and parties) rather than economic institutions (and firms) shape incentives and outcomes. The demand for female representation is powerfully influenced by how effective political party leaders, and indirectly voters, expect female candidates will be. Even in the absence of discriminatory social norms and a voter preference for male politicians, personalistic electoral rules should hurt the electoral chances of female candidates by placing a premium on seniority, career continuity, and individual clout in a way that centralized, party-centered systems do not. By a political analogue to Say's Law, if the demand for female legislators is lower, the supply of qualified female candidates will also be lower. Those who do run are as competitive as male candidates, because they have somehow managed to compensate for institutional disadvantages. But they are a relatively small number.

By contrast, in electoral systems where candidates are elected in large districts and votes are cast for political parties as opposed to individual candidates, party labels (and policy reputation) rather than individual qualities become the deciding factor. Voters still care about the competency of the party as a whole, of course, but such competency will be much more closely associated with party leaders than with individual candidates. And because the critical resource of the party is the party label, party leaders will be more concerned with party discipline than with seniority and cultivating strong candidates. Indeed, the latter may be viewed more as a threat to the party leadership than as an electoral resource. For rank-and-file candidates, being able to commit to long hours and continuous, uninterrupted careers is not a particularly valuable asset in the competition for a spot on the candidate list.

The difference between electoral system and female representation might be stronger if it were not for the fact that majoritarian electoral rules tend to be associated with labor markets that permit the rise of a larger pool of female managers with leadership and managerial experience who may be able inspire voter confidence in their political acumen. Proportional representation systems, by contrast, are associated with production systems that may foster fewer female private sector managers. But large state PR systems are likely to foster women in labor union management and women with a strong interest in promoting public sector employment. The available supply of women with politically relevant talent and experience is therefore uneven across electoral systems, but it strikes us as unlikely that this is the personnel bottleneck that some observers may suppose it to be. Where the labor market for politicians is female-friendly, the supply should be forthcoming but probably somewhat muted in specific skills economies without large public sectors. There may also be an effect of production systems on the *demand* for females that follows from our previous analysis and that we discuss more below. Basically, female candidates may be better able to make credible commitments to "female" issues, and insofar as these are politicized, this may offset other disadvantages. The challenge is to identify the structural limits on the demand for female representation, depending on whether or not career interruption hurts political effectiveness in a given political system. It is ironic, and casts a large shadow on cultural arguments, that majoritarian systems can at once be associated with the most female managers in the private sector but perform so dismally in female political representation. Although at first blush this may also seem to run counter to our labor market structure argument—that is, that some general skills economies perform poorly while some specific skills economies perform well—this not the case if one applies the same logic to the market for politicians.

The Market for Politicians

When effective candidates have to develop long-term ties to their constituents and to other politicians, women are at a disadvantage. Some will, of course, make the necessary sacrifices, but women are less likely to do so, and statistical discrimination—the use of gender as a cue for your vote when information is incomplete—will magnify the problem because parties cannot know the true types, at least among first-term candidates. The bias is affected by two related factors. First, single-member districts, or similar electoral rules that emphasize close ties to constituencies, place a premium on long tenure because the effectiveness of legislators in delivering goods to their constituencies depends on membership in important committees and the ability to make credible bargains with other politicians, both of which are a function of seniority and the prospects of reelection. Because men can more credibly commit to long and continuous careers they are more likely to be elected and reelected, which increases their legislative effectiveness and hence their reelection chances. Second, weak parties mean that individual candidates cannot rely on the party label to lift them above the electoral threshold. Instead they have to cultivate a personal following that again puts a premium on seniority and the accumulation of political capital.[1] In turn, weak political parties are associated with presidential systems where the ability to hold on to executive power does not depend on strong party discipline. Strong parties are instead mostly found in parliamentary systems, except where a single party has such a dominant position that it does not depend on strict discipline (as in the case of the Italian Christian Democrats or the Japanese Liberal Party before the 1990s).

Proportional representation with large districts, or smaller districts where votes are pooled across candidates, produces a very different dynamic that is more conducive to female representation. There is little incentive for individual candidates to cater to local constituencies, and the party label becomes much more important in winning elections than the appeal of individual candidates. Likewise, programmatic parties will place more value on candidate loyalty to the party's platform, which motivates them to nominate and promote politicians with relatively little independent political power—often with an eye to the symbolic value of adhering to such norms as gender equity. Voters always want effective candidates, of course, but what an effective candidate is depends on the political system. Where the party label is of great electoral consequence, women are in no particular disadvantage since representatives (at least the backbenchers) are mostly asked to simply promote policies and vote for them when bills are sent to the floor. Parties can thus respond relatively easily to demands for gender equality, though perhaps less so at the leadership level.

In slightly more formal language, imagine the following two-stage candidate selection game. In the first (nomination) stage, political party leaders select candidates among the available pool of potential candidates to represent their party in the next election. Parties seek to maximize their policy preferences, which is a function of voter support, party discipline (that is, whether members of parliament toe the party line), and effectiveness in legislative bargaining. In the second stage, voters cast their vote for either party programs or individual candidates depending on the electoral system. Voters prefer candidates/parties who are (1) close to their own policy preferences, and (2) reliable (do what they say they will do), and (3) effective in legislative bargaining.

The electoral system constrains the choices of voters and candidates. At one extreme, in closed list systems with a single national district, the party must present a single platform and there is no scope for voters to vote for individual candidates who can deviate from that platform. In this situation, voters care only about the distance between their own policy preferences and the party platform, and the party's effectiveness in advancing it. Any postelection deviations from the platform are a source of uncertainty and a reason not to vote for the party. Anticipating this, the party will put a premium on party loyalty in choosing candidates, whereas effectiveness in legislative bargaining will be a function of the ability of the party leadership to leverage its legislative weight in coalition bargaining with other parties. The result is that the characteristics of rank-and-file candidates become largely irrelevant, except for their fidelity to the party line.

In this institutional setting voters choose parties because of their ability to commit to a desired policy platform (the first stage), and parties in consequence choose candidates to make sure they can deliver on the electoral promises that they make. Assuming that women are no less loyal than men on average, and if both genders are equally capable of credibly committing to certain policies, there is no reason to expect a gender bias in the selection of candidates.[2]

Candidate-centered systems, such as single-member districts (SMD) or the single nontransferable vote (SNTV) system once in place in Japan, are very different because whether a candidate gets elected is likely to depend, at least in some measure, on his or her ability to deliver policies that are favorable to the district. And insofar as individual candidates become guarantors for the pursuit of constituency interests, voters cannot ignore the legislative effectiveness of candidates. Nor, by implication, can the party leadership. Effectiveness in turn derives from innate abilities as well as the bargaining power that comes with being able to never leave the negotiation table, accumulated knowledge about arcane committee procedures, and the opportunity to cultivate a reputation for making credible threats and promises that comes with seniority and uninterrupted political careers. Key to understanding inequality in representation is that men on average have an advantage in accumulating political bargaining power, and hence the ability to deliver constituency goods, because men everywhere enjoy lower average responsibility in caring for young children and elderly parents and in carrying out other family-related duties. This male advantage is what is known to produce inequalities in private labor markets that rely heavily on specialized skills and long tenures,[3] and there are no reasons to suspect that political labor markets should be different.

The implication is not that male candidates are more likely to win elections than female candidates. Since voters have information about the past effectiveness of incumbents, they rationally choose these without regard to gender. The same is true for rookie candidates as long as voters can reasonably assume that parties will pick the best candidates. Since parties have an electoral incentive to do so, this is a rational expectation in the game. But by the same token this implies that parties choose candidates for open seats in a manner that discriminates against women. Specifically, the party will pick those candidates who are close to the party platform and show good potential for being effective in legislative bargaining and for cultivating a personal following. Parties cannot predict the future effectiveness of young candidates with certainty and therefore rely in some measure on imperfect proxies. In particular, they know that men are on average more likely than women to have uninterrupted political careers and to be able to sacrifice family in a manner that is required to build up reputation with constituencies, fellow politicians, and bureaucrats. For this reason, they are more likely to choose men among equally qualified candidates in terms of ability and policy compatibility. The more electoral success relies on ability to cultivate a personal following and curry favors with others, the greater the bias.

The gender bias in the candidate selection process increases the less the party is concerned with party discipline. When party discipline is important for maintaining government power, the discretion of individual legislators may have to be contained. Though some discretion is clearly desirable from an electoral point of view, too much can cause the governing party to lose critical votes in the legislature. This is an aspect of parliamentary systems and much less of a concern in presidential systems where government power does not depend on maintaining a majority in the legislature.[4]

Another complicating factor is that women may be better able credibly to commit to policies that advance the position of women. As in the case of competence, there is an incomplete information problem in terms of voters being confident that the party will implement its policy platform. This may create a gender bias to the extent that issues are gender specific and female candidates can more credibly signal their support for policies that help women balance family and career. If such policies become salient enough for a significant number of women to determine their vote, while the same is not true for men, parties have an incentive to field more female candidates as a way to capture this new group of female swing voters. It is plausible that this dynamic is particularly likely to emerge in countries with labor markets that put women in a distinct disadvantage. In turn, these countries are also the ones that tend to have PR electoral systems.

It is the paradox of welfare states that proportional representation systems tend to suppress private sector female labor force participation, despite the boost to female wages from wage compression, because strong unions tend to create labor markets that penalize career interruptions.[5] The coordinated market economies typical of proportional representation systems tend to organize production in a manner that makes use of long-term labor contracts and specific human capital investments that lose value when broken off by periods of child rearing or other family responsibilities.[6] Firms respond by avoiding hiring or promoting women, and females for their part are less likely to seek jobs that require the long-term, specific investments to which they have difficulty committing.

Government policy, and specifically the hiring of females in public sector jobs, can offset weak private sector demand for female labor, as in the case of the Scandinavian countries. As we showed in chapter 5, the gender voting gap is in fact the largest in countries with the largest public sectors, because in these countries the government provides women not only supplemental help in managing the family-career juggling act but their very jobs.

Majoritarian electoral systems, in contrast to proportional representation systems, tend to undergird liberal market economies (LME) in which labor is forced to adjust to market exigencies more or less on its own and potentially quite frequently. While devastating to the people losing their jobs, fluid labor markets inadvertently help females by reducing employers' incentives to invest in long-term human capital. The demand for female labor in the private sector is higher in proportion to male job insecurity, shorter tenure rates, less restrictive hiring and firing rules, and corporate reliance on mobile, general skills for which there is no or little penalty associated with career interruption. Because women have the market, rather than government policies, to thank for the relatively level playing field they experience, they have less of an interest in pushing for interventionist government policies that subsidize female employment. Because they are redistributive, such policies are more likely to be seen as a matter of class than of gender politics. Though women in LMEs may benefit from policies that further shifted the burdens of family work away from women and increased income equality (women in LMEs still face a significant gender wage gap), the intragender wage inequality in LMEs makes this sort of collective action extremely unlikely. Women at the top of the income ladder have at their disposal private sector alternatives—often supplied by low-paid female workers—to tax-funded child care and other services.

Empirical Analysis

Our empirical analysis falls into two parts. First we test the institutional hypotheses on data from twenty-three advanced democracies beginning in 1945 or at the inception of democracy if later. The dependent variable is the share of seats in national legislatures held by women, using legislative sessions as the unit of observation. Since nearly all the institutional variation is cross-national, the effects of these institutions mainly show up as differences across countries. We do, however, also consider possible explanations for the cross-time trends, and we show that structural forces of change that have driven up female representation everywhere, especially female labor force participation, have been powerfully conditioned by the design of electoral institutions.

We then take advantage of differences in electoral institutions within some countries—either across electoral tiers or across time—to explore whether these appear to affect representation as we would expect. We can exploit this variance as "natural experiments" to test whether women in the same political system do better under some rules than under others. Although the results for a small number of cases can always be challenged on grounds that they are not representative, they can significantly improve our confidence in the causal relationships that are assumed in the large-N analysis.

Large-N Results

Figure 6.1 shows the share of female seats in the lower house of national assemblies across twenty-three democracies and approximately fifty-five years. One is struck by a notable rise in representation over time from an average of about 5 percent immediately following the war to about 25 percent around 2000. But the cross-national differences are also large, and they have been increasing sharply over time. Thus, whereas the range is less than 10 percent in the first observations after the war, in the most recent the female share of representatives varies from a mere 7 percent in Japan to near parity in Sweden.

Clearly the intertemporal variance cannot be explained by changes in political institutions, which have been modest and quite recent where they have occurred, but it is entirely possible that institutional differences have attenuated or magnified the forces of change that have caused female representation to rise everywhere. Along with others we have emphasized two key forces of change in this book. One is entry of women into paid employment caused by the postwar economic boom and the rise of services (as well as the associated rise in divorce rates and public provision of day care). As women enter the labor market they become part of networks and organizations (such as unions) where they are more likely to be exposed to political discussion and advocacy, which in turn encourages interest and involvement in politics. Some will also acquire skills through their work that can be applied in political careers. Although the number of women who end up running for national office is very small, most are recruited among those who are active in the labor market, so representation will likely rise with labor market participation. There may be a significant knock-on effect as women increasingly complete university degrees, which are important assets for launching successful political careers, to prepare themselves for the labor market. So the share of employment held by females should correlate with the share of females in the legislature.

The second force of change is the rise of service employment. The breakdown of patriarchal values during the past half century, documented in this book, is closely linked to the rise of services because these do not depend on physical strength and typically rely more on general than on firm- or industry-specific skills. Since specific skills disadvantage women—

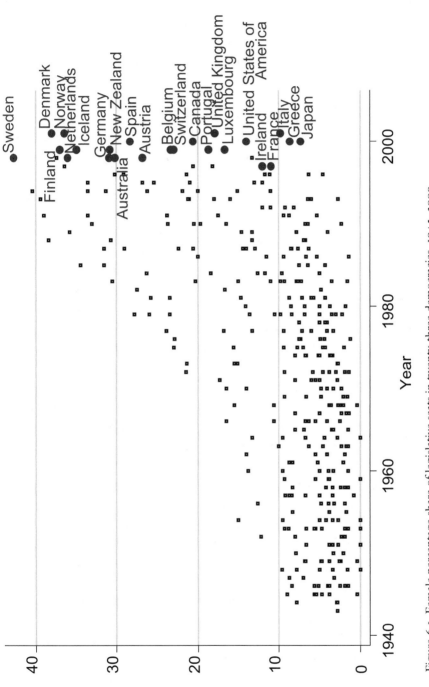

Figure 6.1. Female percentage share of legislative seats in twenty-three democracies, 1945–2000

who cannot as easily commit to uninterrupted careers—and since most services rely on social rather than manual skills, postindustrialization has been a big boon for female labor force participation. But it has also had the effect of equalizing power between the genders and accelerating changes in gender norms. Because women compete on a more equal footing with men for jobs in services than in either manufacturing or agriculture, it has improved women's bargaining position in the family and encouraged caring parents to emphasize values that stress equality in raising their daughters. As boys have been for centuries, girls are increasingly taught to be assertive, acquire a good education, and prioritize financial independence. These values certainly do not lead most women to seek political careers, but they do tend to augment the pool of women from which political candidates will be recruited, and voters are less likely to be prejudiced against female candidates.

The importance of labor market participation and the rise of services for female political representation can be easily ascertained in a model where we control for all cross-national differences using country-specific intercepts (or fixed effects). The results shown at the top of figure 6.2 are based on Prais Winsten estimates with panel-corrected standard errors (Beck and Katz 1995) and correction for first-order autocorrelation (the detailed regression results are reported in table 6.4 in the appendix). The numbers are based on the post-1960 period where we have complete data for all variables and countries. The predicted effect of a 1 percent change in the female share of the labor force is to increase female representation by .41 percent in the long run. The effects of a 1 percent increase in service sector employment are even larger: .74 percent. This implies a 18 percent increase in representation as a result of the actually observed rise in female and service sector employment between the early 1960s (or the first year of democracy) and the late 1990s, which is equal to the actually observed average increase in representation.[7] Service employment appears to have been a particularly important factor, although it is of course highly collinear with female employment.[8]

The rest of figure 6.2 shows the effect of political-institutional variables. Since these are constant (or vary very little) over time we substituted them for the otherwise perfectly collinear fixed effects. Our attention centers on two measures of electoral systems.[9] One is the size of electoral districts, standardized by dividing by the number of seats in the national assembly. The Netherlands is the only country in the data set that treats the entire country as a single electoral district. In this case the value for the district size variable is therefore 1. As the number of candidates elected from each district shrinks, so does the electoral size variable—approaching 0 as we move toward a large number of single-member districts. In cases where the electoral system has more than one tier, the measure is an average district magnitude across tiers weighted by the share of seats elected from each tier.

District size has a very obvious effect on the electoral strategies of political parties that is important to our story. Whereas it makes good sense to field candidates in SMD systems who can cater effectively to local interests, if the electoral district is the nation as a whole, specialization of candidate appeals makes little sense. Even if a party caters to regional interests, or to other narrowly defined constituencies, individual candidates represent the party platform as opposed to their own local or personally cultivated constituencies. In turn, as the focus shifts from individual candidates to party platforms, voters lose interest in the attributes of the former and vote on policies and leadership competency instead.

Another electoral feature that affects the extent to which voters choose parties according to individual candidate qualities as opposed to party platforms is pooling of votes across candidates. If any votes over the required number that a candidate receives are transferred from him or her to other candidates from the same party, voting for a candidate is also in part a vote for the party. This forces voters to pay attention to the party label in addition to individual candidates. How much depends on the specific rules. If votes can be pooled only among subsets of candidates, it still makes sense to pay a lot of attention to individual candidate qualities. If votes are pooled across all party candidates in a district, the party label comes to dominate the qualities of individual candidates in voting decisions, and the party will in consequence choose candidates more because of their ideology and loyalty to the party than their qualifications for cultivating a personal following. We code the variable 1 if votes are pooled across all candidates in a district, 0 if no pooling is allowed, and ½ if pooling is across subsets of candidates.[10] As in the case of the district magnitude variable, if there is more than one tier in the electoral system, the

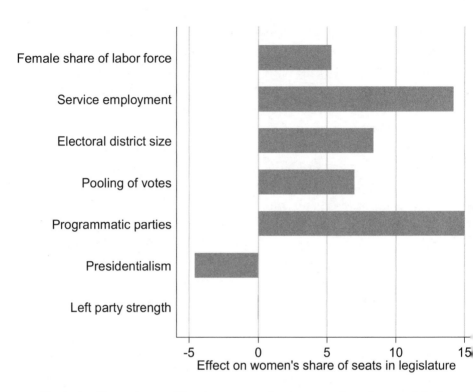

Figure 6.2. Determinants of female representation in twenty-three democratic legislatures, 1960–2000

Note: Effects are calculated based on the regression results reported in table 6.4 in
appendix A. The effects of female share of labor force and service employment is the
estimated effect of the average changes in these variables observed between early
1960s and early 2000s.

measure is an average across tiers weighted by the share of seats elected
from each tier.[11]

The effects of the two electoral variables are in the predicted direction
and quite strong. Moving from the smallest to the largest electoral district
increases the female share of seats in the legislature by an estimated 8 percent, and going from a system with no pooling of votes to one with pooling across all candidates increases female representation by 7 percent. As
it turns out, the effects of the two variables can be almost fully captured
by a simple additive index, which we have labeled "programmatic parties"

(which may be contrasted to "candidate-oriented" parties) in figure 6.2. The estimated total effect of this variable is roughly the same as the sum of the two component variables. Specifically, going from an electoral system with the fewest incentives of parties to compete on party programs (SMD with no pooling) to one where these incentives are the strongest (a single national district with pooling across all candidates) raises the predicted representation of women by 15 percent, all else equal. This difference between electoral systems is greater than the average representation of women in legislatures, which is only 12.2 percent.

The analysis also includes controls for presidentialism and the share of seats in the legislature that are held by left parties.[12] As we noted in the theoretical section, there are long-standing arguments that presidentialism reduces the incentives of parties to enforce adherence to the party label since government power does not depend on maintaining a majority in the legislature. This increases the scope for, and presumably electoral salience of, individual legislators who can strike deals with other legislators through logrolling and other deal making. And, indeed, presidential systems have 4 to 5 percent fewer female representatives, all else being equal, than parliamentary systems. Yet it must be cautioned that since the only two countries in our sample with genuine presidential systems are France and the United States, the presidentialism variable is simply a dummy for those two countries. But both political systems are certainly known to have comparatively weak parties.

While one may reasonably have expected parties on the left to be more sensitive to gender equality, and while that may be true in particular cases, the effect of having higher left party representation is weak and in fact the opposite direction of the expectation. Left parties may have had beneficial indirect effects on female representation through especially female labor force participation—which is partly linked to "women friendly" policies, such as public day care provision, that we discussed in the previous chapter—but they do not appear to have contributed much to improving gender equality in the legislature by advancing women further through their own ranks than other parties.

The final set of results (models [6] and [7] in table 6.4) combines the structural forces of change with the cross-national institutional differences.[13] In one formulation we reintroduce the fixed country effects, but we retain the institutional variable ("programmatic parties") as an interaction term with female labor force participation. All the variance in the dependent variable that can be accounted for by our explanatory variables is now intertemporal, and what the institutional interaction variable tells us is whether pressure for change (represented by an increasing female share of the labor force) is accommodated or hindered in different institutional settings. Indeed, it turns out that institutions do matter. The rate of change in representation in response to higher female employment is almost three times higher in systems with strong incentives for programmatic parties than when these incentives are weak (the coefficient on the female labor force variable rises from .37 to .98). This is confirmed if we omit the country fixed effects and reintroduce the programmatic party variable as an independent predictor. The results are illustrated in figure 6.3.

The figure shows women's predicted share of seats in the legislature as a function of female labor force participation (restricted to the in-sample range) for different values on the programmatic party variable. At low levels of female labor force participation, electoral institutions do not matter much, and we could have anticipated this from figure 6.1. Immediately following World War II there is little variation in female representation, and women were largely outside the labor market. As they gradually enter into paid work, the variance in representation across countries rises. The reason for this divergence, we have suggested, comes down to differences in the design of political institutions, especially electoral rules. Where these motivate parties to compete mainly on programmatic differences in policies, women fare far better than where parties delegate a lot of power and discretion to individual candidates. In the former countries, political gender equality is quickly catching up with economic equality: gender parity in employment is associated with more than 40 percent female representation. In the latter countries, female representation has trouble breaking above 10 percent. The United States is a case in point. Although women have moved toward parity in terms of their share of jobs, they trail men in Congress by a daunting margin. By contrast, women in Sweden have reached virtual parity in both spheres, even though Swedish women started out with fewer than 8 percent of seats in the legislature after the war.

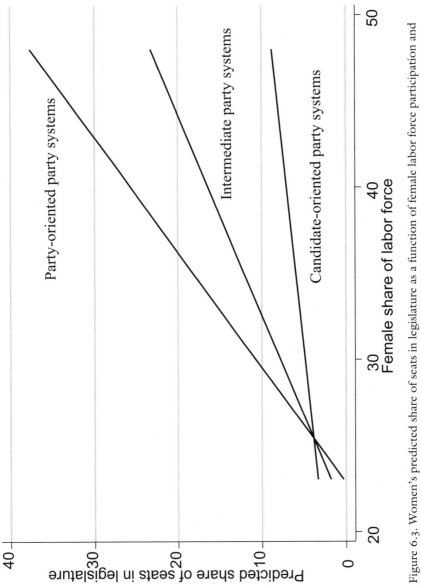

Figure 6.3. Women's predicted share of seats in legislature as a function of female labor force participation and programmatic parties

Female Representation in Five Countries
with Variation in Electoral Rules

Our analysis of cross-national data showed how electoral systems requiring large personal investments in constituency service and reputation disadvantage female candidates. This disadvantage need have no connection to attitudes toward women more generally, but it can be explained by parties' and voters' expectations—similar to the statistical discrimination employers employ in coordinated market economies (CME) labor markets—that females are more likely to interrupt their work, perhaps daily, and interrupt their careers, perhaps for years at a time, to care for their families. In political systems where politicians are expected to "bring home the bacon," voters want representatives whose loyalty and attention is undivided by that other home.

Although the cross-country results are consistent with our claims, they still leave open the possibility that national attitudes toward gender may influence voting behavior independently of the systemic challenges to female political careers posed by different electoral environments that we have emphasized. Adding fixed effects to the model increased the explained variance by 15 to 20 percent, and we cannot be sure that the effects attributed to the mostly invariant electoral rules are not due to unobserved cross-cultural differences.

We can get at the problem of national culture by exploring variation within five countries: Germany, Italy, Japan, New Zealand, and the United States. Because the variation is intracountry, these cases allow us to hold constant cultural values that might color vote choice. They also help exclude the possibility that the low number of female representatives in some countries is due to outright discrimination in the nomination process. The first four cases have mixed electoral systems that allow us to compare the performance of women in contests governed by different electoral rules, and in three cases (Italy, Japan, and New Zealand) there is variance over time that can be treated as "natural experiments." All changed their electoral rules in the 1990s for reasons that were almost certainly unrelated to issues of gender inequality. The United States is also a useful case for us because of the availability of data at different levels of government and because the relatively high levels of female labor force participation, even in the ranks of senior management, suggest openness to female leadership. The mismatch between women's high visibility in the economy and their low political profile in the United States presents a genuine puzzle for arguments that emphasize cultural dispositions about gender roles. We exploit differences in career continuity and professionalization across levels of government in the United States, given that turnover tends to be higher in local than in national government. If our argument about office-specific investments is right, we expect women to be more disadvantaged at higher levels of government where terms tend to be longer than for lower office.

Germany, Italy, Japan, and New Zealand: Laboratories of Natural Experimentation

Countries with mixed electoral systems provide periodic snapshots of the likelihood of females to get elected, holding constant everything but the type of seat being filled for office. For our purposes, the perfect natural experiment would be for each voter to have two ballots, one for each of two types of seats that epitomize the extreme cases of personalistic and party competition. We would expect any given voter, irrespective of his or her gender biases and prejudices, to be less likely to vote for female candidates for district-based seats in which seniority and career continuity are more important for office performance than in list seats that are controlled by the party leadership and where the party label is much more important to voters. Party leaders and candidates, knowing the premium on career continuity in district-based systems, respond to the demand by disproportionately supplying men in those positions.[14]

No such perfect experiment exists because party discipline, which in mixed systems is the product of some weighted average between two types of party backbenchers, reins in the personalism of district-based candidates.[15] Specifically, when there is a need for party discipline in one type of seat that constrains the freedom of candidates in the other type of seat, voters in the latter have to pay more attention to the party label, which reduces the male advantage in those seats. Nonetheless, different electoral incentives persist to some degree across two types of seats in Germany, Italy, Japan, and New Zealand, providing approximations of the experiment conditions we have in mind.

Table 6.1. District type and female representation in Germany, 1945–2005; standard errors in parentheses

	(1)	*(2)*
Female share of labor force	2.44***	1.86***
	(0.35)	(0.45)
Left party strength (percent seats controlled by left)	0.225**	0.227**
	(10.72)	(10.17)
Party list seat (as opposed to constituency seat)	11.39***	(5.04)
	(3.14)	(4.43)
Female share of labor force × party list	—	1.18*
		(0.62)
Adj. R-squared	0.818	0.847
N	30	30
Rho	0.70	0.70

Key: *p < .10; **p < .05; ***p < .01 (two-tailed tests)

In each of these countries, the share of women winning representation on lists is 8 to 16 percent higher than the share from districts. Since the average female share of seats is always significantly below 50 percent, this difference translates into a much higher probability that a woman will be nominated and elected in a list-based seat. In Germany, for example, the proportion getting elected in list seats is more than twice that of constituency seats. This is a striking difference, given that district-based candidates in mixed systems are constrained by the rest of the party in the degree to which they can run personal electoral machines.

Germany offers the most comprehensive evidence for our thesis since the dual-ballot system has been in place since the end of World War II. German voters are confronted with two ballots, one for the local single-member constituency (coded 0) and one for a party list (coded 1), where the overall allocation of seats is proportional to the number of list votes. This unique electoral system enables us to run regressions that are analogous to those used to generate the electoral system results in the previous section. Model (1) in table 6.1 explains female representation as a function of the share of women in the labor force, left party strength, and seat type; model (2) adds an interaction between female share of the labor force and seat type.[16] Since GDP per capita is almost perfectly collinear with the female share of the labor force (r = .98), we had to drop it (and the presidentialism variable is obviously no longer relevant). As before we ran a cross-section time-series model on the data, where the two district types are treated as sections.

The results are very similar to those for the cross-national sample. Female participation in paid employment also raises women's share of seats in the legislature, and women are much more likely to be elected in a party list seat than in a single-member constituency seat. The average estimated difference between the two seat types is 11.4 percent, which is equivalent to 85 percent of the average representation of women in the German legislature. This is slightly smaller than the effect of electoral institutions we found in the cross-national analysis (125 percent), but it is obviously still a very sizable effect.

The findings for the interactive model, where the effect of changes in female labor force participation is conditional on the type of seat, are also very similar to the analogous findings for the cross-national regression (figure 6.3, above). When women make up the smallest observed share of the labor force (which is set to 0 in the regression), the difference in seat type is fairly small (5 percent), whereas for the highest observed share, the difference is large (18 percent). Just as countries with PR institutions and strong programmatic parties are more sensitive to the economic mobilization of women, so is the representation of women in the list seats of the German two-ballot system when compared to the constituency seats. The pattern is identical to that illustrated in figure 6.3, above, except that the effects are somewhat smaller—precisely as predicted by the electoral system and party discipline arguments. The only other notable difference in the results is that left parties are associated with a somewhat higher, and statistically significant, representation of women (whereas there is no effect in the cross-national sample). Since the main nonsocialist party is the Christian Democrats, it is conceivable that this is an effect of a more conservative view on women by that party.

In the cases of Italy, Japan, and New Zealand, since mixed electoral systems were introduced only after 1994 (abolished again in 2005 in Italy), the number of legislative sessions is too small to replicate the German re-

Table 6.2. Percent women elected to the national legislature by type of seat (Italy, Japan, New Zealand)

	List seats	*Constituency seats*	*Difference*
Italy	10.4	7.8	2.6
Japan	11.2	4.4	6.8
New Zealand	37.8	22.5	15.3
Germany	19.5	7.6	11.9

Note: Legislative assembly coverage: Italy: 1994, 1996, 2001; Japan: 1996, 2000, 2003, 2005; New Zealand: 1996, 1999, 2002, 2005.

gression analysis. Instead, table 6.2 simply shows the average differences in the share of women elected in different types of seats in each country, including Germany for comparison. In every case, and in fact in every election (there are a total of eleven under mixed rules), the share of women elected from list seats exceeds the share of women elected from constituency seats. The difference is modest in the case of the Italian Senate, but even there the list portion of the ballot returns nearly a third more women than constituency races.

It is hard to think of an explanation for the pattern in table 6.2 without recourse to differences in the incentives built into the electoral rules. The German pattern could perhaps be attributed to special circumstances that existed after World War II, though it is not clear which—or why these would have persisted. But the mixed systems that were introduced very recently in the other three countries show the same tendency.

One conceivable explanation might be that the nomination process for constituency seats has greater input from local politicians who are more socially conservative than national politicians. But if this were true, the difference between list and constituency seats should disappear in urban districts where voters are socially liberal. That is not the case. Instead the results add up to strong evidence, we think, of lower voter demand for, and lower party and candidate supply of, female representatives in the kind of seat in which long-term constituency service is vital for electoral success.

We can further explore the effects of electoral design by examining how

Table 6.3. Actual and predicted change in female representation as a result
of electoral reform

	(1) Actual change	*(2)* Predicted effect of electoral change	*(3)* Predicted effect of other variables	*(4)* Total predicted change *(2) + (3)*
Italy	2.5 (1.7)	−1.9	1.7	−0.2
Japan	5.6 (6.3)	4.1	4.4	8.5
New Zealand	13.9 (11.0)	6.7	4.4	11.2

female representation in the legislature responds to institutional reform.
The change we would expect in the three cases where such reforms occurred is simply the difference across seat type recorded in table 6.2 times
the share of total seats elected under a new formula, where the direction
of change depends on whether the reform is from a candidate-oriented
system toward a party-oriented system, or vice versa. For example, in the
case of New Zealand about 44 percent of the 120 MPs have been elected
on party lists starting with the 1996 election. The rest have been chosen
through the old SMD method. Since the (average) difference in female
representation between the two systems is 15.3 percent (see table 6.2) we
would expect the net effect of electoral reforms to be an increase in female representation of $0.44*15.3 = 6.7$ percent. This is the figure shown
in column (2) of table 6.3. The actual increase was 13.9 percent (column
1). Much of this gap, however, can be accounted for by the fact that other
factors affecting female representation also changed. Although we do not
know the identity of all these factors in each case, we can use the cross-national results to predict their effect based on observed changes in the share
of the labor force that is female, changes in per capita income, and changes
in the representation of left parties in the legislature—while assuming that
electoral institutions remain the same. This is the estimated counterfac-

tual in column (3) (based on model [7] from table 6.4 in the appendix). In all cases we use the means for the postreform period and compare the numbers to the means for the equivalent number of legislative assemblies before the reform.

In the case of New Zealand, the total predicted change in representation from electoral reforms and exogenous factors (11.2) is very close to the actual observed change (13.9). In the other two cases there is either "too little" or "too much" observed change compared to the prediction. Thus while improvement in female representation in Italy has been very slow, the predicted change is actually slightly negative because of electoral reforms that are disadvantageous to women. It is noteworthy, however, that with the return to a pure PR list system in 2005—and this time to a system without preferential voting—women's representation in the Senate almost doubled (from 7.9 to 13.7 percent). Structural forces of changes are clearly driving up the number of women elected to national office in Italy, but they have almost certainly been subdued by the "majoritarian" interlude from 1994 to 2005.

The pattern in Japan is the mirror image of Italy. Here electoral reforms should have benefited women, and the same should be true for the notable increases in incomes and growing female labor force participation. Yet actual changes have been less impressive: 5.6 compared to the prediction of 8.5. But it takes time to reach the equilibrium, and if we look at the period since the electoral reforms, women representation in the Diet has in fact increased sharply from 3.7 percent in 1993 to 9 percent in 2005—more than a doubling. If we compare the last observation under the new rules to the last on the old rules—under the assumption that changes take time as a result of incumbency advantages—actual changes (noted in parentheses in column 1 of table 6.3 above) are closer to the predicted (6.3 versus 8.5). Such convergence between observed and predicted changes can also be seen in the other two cases. All in all, the cross-time evidence from the three cases clearly supports the cross-seat evidence.

The United States: Levels of Government and the Effects of Turnover Rates

Women in the United States are represented in greater numbers at lower levels of government, and the number of female politicians shrinks on the way up the political pyramid.[17] One might infer from this that Americans are ready for women to represent them in local or state office but not in national government where more is at stake. Our argument, instead, is that lower political offices in the United States are more like general skills labor markets where labor markets are fluid and the probability of career continuity is of lesser advantage. Local and state legislative jobs are characterized by high turnover compared to House and Senate seats. Relatively few politicians settle into careers on the city council; rather they plan to keep moving up the ladder. For political positions characterized by short-term careers, a female candidate who might quit in a few years to raise her children or to care for elderly parents is not dramatically different than a male candidate with sights on higher office or a private sector career.[18]

Female politicians in the United States seem to have internalized the logic of political labor markets, for they self-select into offices with higher turnover. The result is dramatic attrition of females on the way up the political pyramid, as incumbents have fewer lures to move them along and political tenure grows longer. In 2006, 15.4 percent of the U.S. House of Representatives was female, compared with 22.8 percent female in state legislatures. Lower down at the county and town level, the percentage of women tends to be even higher. In New Jersey, for example, which has no women in its congressional delegation, 27.7 percent of local commissioners were women. The pyramidical structure of female representation is similar in England, where 19.7 percent of the House of Commons is female compared to 27 percent of local councils.[19]

The contrast with the proportional representation systems in Europe is striking. There, party leaders choose candidates to higher office for party loyalty rather than voters choosing them on the basis of district loyalty and visibility, with the result that career interruption need not pull female politicians out of the queue for higher office. Rather than the pyramid we find in the United States and United Kingdom, the structure of female representation in Sweden, for example, is a column: 45.3 percent in the national parliament, 47.3 percent in county councils, and 42.4 percent in municipal councils.[20]

Conclusions

Given that women have been subjected to unfavorable stereotyping and second-class treatment for as long as history has kept track, outright discrimination would seem a reasonable explanation for why women are less likely than men to get elected to political office. We might expect that a shift in societal values toward greater gender egalitarianism would contribute to a rise in female labor force participation and a concurrent rise in female political representation. In rich democracies, particularly in the post–World War II decades, women have indeed cut into male hegemony in labor markets as well as in politics. The correlation between the two phenomena is consistent with "demand side" theories that stress general attitudinal change, and with "supply side" theories about the relevance of labor market skills and experience for political candidacy.

While there is much truth to these stories about changes in voter reception of female candidacy, the correlation between female success in labor markets and in politics fails to account for enormous cross-national variation in female political representation. In some countries, such as in Scandinavia, female labor force participation and female political representation are powerfully correlated, whereas in other countries, such as the United States, the slope of the curve is much flatter.

Our explanation for the gender gap in representation is very simple and uses the same logic for political careers that we know drives gender inequality in other careers. When jobs require uninterrupted tenures and long inflexible schedules, women are at a distinct disadvantage. Political parties in advanced democracies may have an ambition to encourage gender equality in representation, but just like firms competing in product markets, they are sometimes constrained by electoral competition to put up candidates who are in a strong position to produce specialized constituency goods that require a long tenure and round-the-clock presence. The pool of qualified candidates for that type of job overrepresents men, whether that job is in politics or in private enterprise. By contrast, where parties mainly compete on party labels there is no reason to prefer male over female candidates, at least for filling rank-and-file positions in the party. Ideological commitment and party loyalty are general qualities that do not differ systematically by gender.

The case of the United States, where the ascent of women into middle management is not matched by female success in politics, illustrates our argument. American labor markets are characterized by an abundance of general skills jobs, for which women are competitive. The same is not true of congressional jobs. The reason, we have argued, is that the personalistic qualities of the American political system cause the same cast of characters—the American public—to make considerably less egalitarian choices in the ballot box than in the market place.

Appendix A: Cross-National Regression Results

Table 6.4. The determinants of female representation in twenty-three democratic legislatures, 1960–2000; standard errors in parentheses

	(1)	(2)	(3)	(4)	(5)	(6)	(7)
Female share of labor force	0.41** (0.10)	0.18* (0.07)	0.62** (0.09)	0.83** (0.09)	0.82** (0.08)	0.37** (0.10)	0.22** (0.12)
Service employment as pct of working age pop.	0.72** (0.09)	0.23** (0.05)	—	—	—	—	—
GDP per capita ('000 dollars)	—	—	0.50** (0.06)	0.36** (0.06)	0.37** (0.06)	0.50** (0.06)	0.44** (0.06)
Electoral district size	—	—	—	8.36** (1.41)	—	—	—
Pooling of votes	—	—	—	6.98** (0.85)	—	—	—
Presidentialism	—	—	—	-4.59** (1.08)	-4.43** (1.07)	-5.67** (2.47)	-3.04** (0.93)

Left party strength (percent seats controlled by left)	—	—	—	−0.04* (0.02)	−0.04* (0.02)	−0.03 (0.02)	−1.13 (1.95)
Programmatic parties	—	—	—	—	7.36** (0.69)	—	−1.53 (1.26)
Female share of labor force × programmatic parties	—	—	—	—	—	0.29** (0.04)	0.64** (0.08)
Lagged dependent variable	—	0.77** (0.06)	—	—	—	—	—
Adj. R-squared	0.878	0.949	0.874	0.681	0.682	0.895	0.714
N	244	241	266	249	249	249	249
No. of countries	21	21	23	23	23	23	23
Fixed effects	Yes	Yes	Yes	No	No	Yes	No
Correction for AR-1	Yes	No	Yes	Yes	Yes	Yes	Yes
Rho	0.47	—	0.49	0.78	0.76	0.47	0.64

Key: *p < .05; **p < .01 (two-tailed tests)

7

CONCLUSIONS

Women, given that they make up half of the human race, are a heterogeneous group of people with as much to divide as to unite them. It would be inappropriate to write a book about them at all if it were not for a striking similarity in social attitudes toward women's roles throughout most of the world and over most of human history. A woman is to be a faithful wife and a good mother. Faithful husband and good father rank high on the list for men in most societies as well, but they come lower on the list for males than for females and are invariably preceded by other mandates, such as to be strong, brave, and successful in the world of men.

We do not wish to be read as saying that women are poor and oppressed while men are joyful and triumphant. The pressures on males to be strong, brave, and successful themselves constitute a heavy psychic burden, no doubt contributing to the shorter male life span. In addition to being vulnerable to modern stress-related diseases, men have always been more likely to die in war and from work-related injuries. Our point is rather that the long-standing economic division of labor in which females stay at home while men work in the world has the effect of weakening women's bargaining power at home and of creating social norms that reinforce male dominance in most spheres of human life.

In modern democracies, the starkly gendered division of labor is crumbling and gender equality is now the only politically correct stance on the subject. But there is still considerable variation in equality in practice, and understanding that variation provides leverage on the remaining inequality. We hope for a time when a book such as this one is categorized as history, but that time has not yet arrived. This is especially true in developing countries where patriarchy is as entrenched as it has always been in many cases. We hope our argument will be used and tested in these settings where, we believe, male dominance is all too often attributed to culture.

Summarizing the Argument

Patriarchy, we have argued, is the combined result of myriad strategic decisions by parents to socialize their daughters for the marriage market rather than for the labor market in light of an economic system for which marketable female labor is not as productive as male's. Most of these decisions were undoubtedly not strategic at all, at least in the sense of conscious efforts to maximize utility. Rules of thumb that work for one generation get passed along to subsequent ones, and as long as they work, they tend to become enshrined in moral and religious teachings. Put economistically, social norms about gender roles enabled people to economize on information about choices over education, marriage, and work and helped them avoid making potentially costly errors.

The resulting enormous differences in the allocation of social resources across the sexes were out of all proportion to the small average difference in physical size between the sexes. There were surely many egregious cases of inefficient use of resources, where strong women stayed at home while weak men struggled with ox and plow. But social norms are most powerful when they are generalized as rules, and so the trade-off was made. There were also many efficiency-improving variations on the theme, such as where a weaker division of labor emerged under conditions of land abundance. The brawn advantage weakens with land abundance because the labor inputs are a smaller piece of the equation and raise the marginal product of labor. But on balance, we suggest, the gendered division of labor became ubiquitous because it was efficient, creating gains from trade within families when technology was not an available substitute for brawn.

The power of norms to outlive the economic circumstances from which they sprang is most visible when the arrival of technology is met, as in the case of Victorian England, with a retrenchment of gender roles. Analogously to the staged celebration of political absolutism after the French Revolution, those threatened by a blurring of traditional gender roles sought to draw the lines between the sexes even more firmly. Moral and religious education added to the tensile strength of social norms by attaching cosmic significance to what otherwise might have been simple economic choices. Although efficiency is a tough competitor to beat in the very long run, moralizers and other incumbents have been able to manipulate social norms for an effective eternity for any given generation of women.

Changes in the relative productivity of male and female labor under different modes of economic production explain the broad arc of gender socialization by way of changes in the bargaining power of women inside the home. Demand for female labor confers on females the ability to leave unsatisfactory marriages, which in turn translates into women's bargaining leverage within the household. We do not suggest, like Engels, that all marriages are bad and should be abolished. On the contrary, the declining economic gains from marriage highlight the nonmaterial reasons for marriage, including mutual love and respect. But for the relationships in which these break down, divorce more easily results. The rise of the service economy has set in motion an avalanche of changes as more women enter the labor market, divorce rates increase, and girls are taught independence over subservience. We have optimistically proposed that these changes mark a shift toward a more gender-egalitarian equilibrium, but we have also suggested that they are accompanied by a growing gender gap in political preferences as well as unsustainable low fertility rates. In addition, subtle differences in labor market conditions across modern democracies explain another striking pattern. In economies dominated by long-term labor contracts, the expected productivity of female labor is discounted by the probability that females will leave the job before the employer has reaped the full value of its investment in their human capital. As a result, female labor force participation is lower in these countries, except where large public sectors—as in Scandinavia—account for a large portion of female employment. There are in fact multiple gender equilibria corresponding to distinct varieties of capitalism.

Female bargaining power, measured in our empirical investigation by the proportion of household work they do over and above what is predicted by labor market participation alone, is stronger in countries with fluid labor markets and where public sector employment is large enough to offset the negative effects of long-term contracts on female employment in the private sector. Where barriers to divorce cut off a possible marital exit, demand for female labor has a muted effect on female bargaining power.

In rich democracies, the same factors that confer household bargaining power on women also have a positive effect on fertility. We interpret this to mean that women would like to "have it all" as long as having children does not block their possibilities of accumulating human capital in the labor market. Trying to boost fertility with a campaign of pro-family rhetoric and incentives is likely to have precisely the opposite effect as intended. This is an important lesson to democracies in especially southern Europe and East Asia where traditionalist views on women and the family are increasingly in conflict with the desire of, and opportunities for, women to have independent careers. We surmise that this tension will eventually translate into a significant gender gap in voting and a shift in government policies. Indeed, this may already be playing itself out in a country like Spain where the Zapatero government has taken on the Catholic Church over issues of family policy and where women voted disproportionately for the incumbent Socialist Party.

But female bargaining power in the family does not always have the effect, as one might expect, of also boosting female political representation. While it is true that higher levels of female labor market participation creates a gender voting gap between male and female voters that parties may try to exploit by fielding female candidates, the nature of the political labor market itself blocks such a simple connection between potential demand and supply of female candidates. As with labor markets in the economy, political labor markets characterized by long-term contracts—or a premium on seniority—disadvantage female candidates. In electoral rules where personal political clout is an important asset, relatively few females can match males' unfettered ability to accumulate political capital early and continuously through their careers. In proportional representation systems, where party loyalty supplants individual visibility in importance, women are able to compete on more equal footing and do far better in electoral races.

New Research Frontiers

An analysis based on the interaction of household bargaining with modes of production explains some mysteries but opens up still others for future inquiry. We speculate about three of them here briefly: the processes of norm formation and change, the effects of representation by female politicians, and the possibilities of squaring gender equality with global economic competition.

The line we draw between the relative productivity of male versus female labor, on one hand, and gender norms, on the other, runs through a complex series of individual cognitive processes, interpersonal bargaining (explicit or implicit), intergenerational socialization, and macrosocial adaptations that are only dimly understood in modern social science. We find indirect evidence that strategic opportunities motivate families to steer their children in response, but we know far less about how family decisions agglomerate into community-wide normative structures, and still less about when individuals are willing to be guided by societal rules of thumb rather than to evaluate strategic circumstances on their own.[1] Our model of norm change assumes that when faced with attractive enough opportunities, people will endure social opprobrium to reap economic benefits, but we have only a vague idea about the exchange rate between economic gain and social disfavor and about what factors shape this exchange rate across societies and for types of people. The fertility crisis in a range of countries with entrenched patriarchal norms illustrates the point. It seems to suggest a profound shift in female preferences in favor of having careers over families despite the centrality of the family in religious and cultural norms. No one could, or did, predict how women would choose in this trade-off (even though we can identify factors that affect the severity of the trade-off).

Political representation is a second important area of inquiry that we only scratch on the surface. We have a fairly well-developed idea of why female political representation varies, but we understand less well the consequences of female representation and by what mechanisms. If representatives are good agents of their voting constituents, only the voters' preferences should matter and not the personal preferences of the representative. Although there is some evidence that female-led town councils in India press for different outcomes than male-dominated councils, it is not clear why the male-dominated councils are unresponsive to the needs of half of their voters and if that result would be replicated elsewhere. There is a host of questions embedded here: how is the representation of "women's interests" affected by the competitiveness of elections, the quality of information, the self-awareness of women as voters, the priority of women-specific issues among other electorally salient issues? When are female politicians more likely to share the preferences of women voters? Which preferences? Of which women? If female representatives are chosen by parties to capitalize on the gender voting gap, when are female politicians at a critical mass to affect policies? How would the number of women in parliament matter apart from the parties' electoral strategies?[2] A deeper understanding of these issues will provide a better road map for formulating and implementing more gender-friendly policies, including the vexing question of quotas.

The third issue we have raised but not settled is whether gender equality is consistent with economic globalization. Is gender equality efficient? A precise answer to this question would require more data than are currently available to evaluate the costs and benefits for all societal actors of abandoning a gendered division of labor. Even if we had the data, we would then struggle to choose an algorithm for calculating the result, since political philosophy offers no universally agreed metric for weighing interpersonal utilities.

We are left with the less elegant but more manageable task of considering the trade-offs entailed in making different policy choices. Liberal market economies managed to achieve relatively high gender equality, surely inadvertently, by keeping labor markets fluid in ways that did not put women at a disadvantage against men. Class inequality is the greater problem than gender equality in those countries. There are more female managers in those economies than in the more generous welfare states, but income inequality is stark among women as well as among men. It is also true that women tend to cluster in the low-skill jobs at the bottom of the wage dispersion. In the past the family compensated for this inequality to some extent because higher-earning males were more likely to marry lower-earning females. This pattern has now reversed in that economically successful men now are much more likely to marry equally successful women, increasing the inequality in the distribution of family income. This trend is magnified by a higher probability of low-income females ending up as single mothers. The challenge in these countries with short-term job commitments is therefore to improve the life chances of men and women without means, and especially low-income single parent families, by increasing opportunities for skill acquisition and retraining as necessary.

Scandinavian countries tackled gender equality without sacrificing class equality, also inadvertently. Expanded public sectors created enormous demand for female employment while also providing social insurance against poverty. Whether large public sectors are consistent with economic competition and integration depends in part on whether the voting publics are willing to pay taxes out of wages in order to keep corporate taxes at globally competitive rates, and so far they have been more or less willing to do that. Without doubt this is facilitated by centrally coordinated wage-setting systems, which facilitate wage solidarism and keep up wages in low-skill services that are sheltered from international competition while holding down wages in internationally traded goods and services. This produces relatively highly priced services (partly reflected in taxes) but is fully compatible with high international competitiveness when coupled with public investment in training.[3]

The coordinated market economies of continental Europe and Japan unintentionally hurt women when they protected labor from layoffs, because women cannot compete with men in committing credibly to human capital accumulation over long careers. Although female political representation tends to be higher in these countries than in the district-based systems of liberal market economies, gender-friendly policies have not yet made much of a dent in many outcomes of concern to women, such as female employment, the gender wage gap, male share of household work, and the ability to have children without negative career effects. Adverse labor market conditions amount to an uphill battle that women have not yet won in many of the most developed countries in the world. But as the fertility crisis suggests, this may not be a sustainable situation. If women are not having children because they want careers, rising demand for government policies that facilitate female labor force participation, if our results are correct, cannot be far behind.

In all of these rich democracies, demand for female labor is potentially as high as demand for male labor. No longer is brawn a consideration, and foregoing female brains to reach lower in the male barrel is an economic cost. The reason that long-term labor contracts hurt females—in private sector labor markets in Europe and Japan and in politics in district-based electoral systems—is simply that women are still doing a disproportionate amount of the family work. As long as females are the default caregivers, they face an uneven playing field.

Conclusions

Patriarchy is gasping for breath in the developed world, but it is still with us. In the developing world where the primary sector still dominates the economy, patriarchy is alive and well. The good news for women is that economic development generates a demand for female labor and thereby gives them exit options to oppressive relationships. But this is cold comfort for the many women facing decades before their economies reach that stage of development. In democracies in the developing world, female voters may seek government help in bearing the costs of family work, but many of those countries have electoral rules that make it exceedingly difficult for women to attain office in the first place. Those that do struggle to build coalitions in favor of the measures needed to overcome the extremely adverse market conditions that women face in poor democracies.

Life for women is getting better, but women are not yet equal citizens. Until it becomes a commonplace that fathers are as responsible for the care of children and home as mothers, markets will discriminate against women. Although this is more true in labor markets characterized by long-term contracts than elsewhere, it is true to some degree everywhere. It is time for men to share the same burdens and joys of family work. Judging from mortality statistics, less pressure to be strong, brave, and successful might do a man good.

Chapter 1. A Political Economy Approach to Gender Inequality

1. We agree with the basic tenet of feminism that "many of the characteristics traditionally attributed to either women or men on the basis of biology are more general human characteristics whose identification as 'feminine' or 'masculine' is a matter of social belief." McCloskey 1993, 10.

2. Esping-Andersen wrote his 1999 book largely in response to a critique by Ann Orloff (1993) that his earlier work on the welfare state lacked attention to gender inequality and the family. Other work in the macrosociological literature includes O'Connor, Orloff, and Shaver (1999) and Huber and Stephens (2000).

3. Feminist political economy shows how cultural blinders such as patriarchy shape individual beliefs through internalized norms. To name a few, Inglehart and Norris (2003) discuss the power of society-wide values and value changes on gender and other issues; Catharine MacKinnon (1983) describes the hegemony of male views of sexuality and power; Allan Johnson (1997) shows how social values create a male need to control; Deirdre McCloskey (2003) argues that the concept of "efficiency" itself is a largely male concoction. Macrolevel approaches may also focus on how market structures shape behavior through incentives, such as the work by Milkman, Reese, and Roth (1998) that shows how different levels of income inequality affect the availability of employment to men versus women.

4. Gary Becker's work is the locus classicus for the microeconomic point of view, arguing that household division of labor produces gains from trade. There is also a burgeoning literature on the effects of division of labor on the woman's bargaining power, including, for example, McElroy and Horney 1981, Lundberg and Pollak 1996, Braunstein and Folbre 2001, and an excellent summary of the literature in Lundberg and Pollak 2001.

5. For simplicity, we are considering heterosexual unions and calling them marriages even if they are informal forms of cohabitation.

6. It is also undoubtedly true, as an anonymous reviewer pointed out, that women have more time for political participation in countries where they have less demanding jobs. But that is an incomplete explanation, since the availability of demanding jobs has not hurt male political careers. Indeed, as Kenworthy and Malami (1999) point out, voters seem to prefer candidates with managerial experience.

7. There is a lively debate between "naturists" and "nurturists" on the effects of parenting on child development. See, e.g., Judith Rich Harris 1998; John Bowlby 1951, 1990.

8. Baker and Jacobsen 2007; we are grateful to Shelly Lundberg for alerting us to this insight.

9. See, e.g., Donald McCloskey 1993.

10. Kuhn and Stiner (2001) suggest that Homo sapiens may have outcompeted Neanderthals by developing a division of labor within the family that better used available resources. Whereas Neanderthal communities hunted together, Homo sapiens males specialized in hunting and the females in gathering. Even if this is true, this early division of labor had minimal distributional consequences since Homo sapiens females at that time still had access to their own means of livelihood.

11. Materialism encompasses the neoclassical belief in market forces in its various forms, such as factors of production (land, capital, labor, and human capital) or sectoral and firm-specific interests. It also includes the Marxian belief that classes are the relevant players on account of material interests that hold them together and drive them to collide. The main difference among these arguments is the appropriate level of aggregation, which rests on different implicit or explicit theoretical underpinnings about where collective action problems lie and what sorts of circumstances are likely to overcome them.

12. Note the similarity to Foucault's argument about efficient forms of punishment under different modes of production: hurting the body if brawn is the currency, taking away a criminal's time if wage labor is the currency. The costs and available technologies of enforcement determined the severity of punishment in each case. Posner (1985) picked up on this latter point in his article about optimal deterrence and the criminal law, arguing that prison was needed in cases where perpetrators couldn't afford to pay the fines needed to deter them. We are grateful to Ian Shapiro for pointing these points out to us.

13. See Cusack, Iversen, and Soskice 2007.

14. This is true even among women with working-class backgrounds who tend to be outside unions.

Chapter 2. The Structure of Patriarchy

1. Keohane 1980, 139.

2. Rousseau certainly was chauvinistic. He insisted that his housekeeper/common law wife put their five children in the foundling home. But he was not alone; the foundling homes were crowded to overflowing.

3. In drawing the causal arrow from material conditions to social norms, our argument has much in common with the structuralist "gender stratification theory" in

the field of sociology (Collins 1971; Blumberg 1984; Collins et al. 1993; Blumberg 2004), though there are differences. Collins's initial theoretical argument focused on male physical coercive power. Blumberg broadened the gender stratification theory to include the way relative economic productive power and kinship systems enable or disable autonomous female action. We argue that women themselves benefited, at least in the sense of constrained optimization.

4. Paternity uncertainty is a peculiarly male problem. Females would have had mixed incentives: on one hand, they would maximize resources to their young if they could assure their mates of their children's paternity. On the other hand, they would also have a biological incentive to mate with the best genetic material they could find and pass the offspring off as their mate's. Social rules have been devised to increase the costs of this cheating.

5. Trivers (1971) formalized the Darwinian argument that the parent with the higher investment in reproduction should be choosier about mates. Adrienne Zilhmann (1989) extends the logic to conclude that female choosiness should confer a reproductive advantage on male traits such as nurturing and kindness that females desire for the fathers of their offspring.

6. Gary Becker is best known for this argument: 1964, 1965, 1971, 1981, 1985.

7. Braunstein and Folbre 2001; Lundberg and Pollak 1996.

8. See the appendix to this chapter for a formalization of this logic in terms of a Rubinstein bargaining game.

9. This implies that the game is in fact a dynamic one because the endowment of assets, which depends on specialization, is partly a function of prior choices by the household members. We discuss this issue in greater depth in the appendix.

10. This logic also points to a motivation that is difficult to separate from bargaining power: insurance against divorce. The more likely a marriage is to end in divorce, the greater the incentive to cultivate outside options by investing in marketable assets.

11. Iversen, Rosenbluth, and Soskice (2005).

12. In principle this requires a dynamic representation of the game, but the effect can be indirectly captured by a higher propensity of a woman to participate when others do.

13. This is not strictly speaking true because there is no possibility of conflict of interest, or bargaining, in the Becker model.

14. See, e.g., Leacock 1978; Zihlman 1989; Du 2002.

15. Hawkes 1993; Hill and Hurtado 1997; Hrdy 1981, 1999; Pinker 1997.

16. Divale and Harris (1976) found a statistical connection between the prevalence of warfare and female infanticide, presumably because the status of males rises with the importance of the male comparative advantage in physical protection. But Kristin Hawkes (1981, 83) showed that there was substantial variation in infanticide between warring societies with and without patrilocal living arrangements. "While the warring societies as a whole have an average junior sex ratio of 126:100 it is the patrilocal component of the sample which produces the bias while the nonpatrilocal component shows a nearly even sex ratio."

17. Low 2000.

18. Studying the Middle East, Blaydes and Linzer (2008) and Michael Ross (2008) provide evidence that women are more likely to be religious fundamentalists in countries with lower female labor force participation.

19. Goldin (1991).

20. Geddes and Lueck (2002).

21. Iversen and Rosenbluth 2006; Iversen, Rosenbluth, and Soskice 2005.

22. Brinton 2007.

23. See Iversen and Soskice 2001 for details. It may be objected that since occupational distribution of workers has changed since the introduction of ISCO-88 the skill specialization of each group may simply reflect the depletion of some groups and expansion of others. The patterns present below, however, are very similar if we instead use employment data from the 1980s.

24. The two occupations where women are the most overrepresented ("clerks" and "service and sales workers") are also relatively low skill, but this is not true for the next two groups where women are (relatively) overrepresented ("professionals" and "technicians and associated professionals"). So the relationship in Figure 2.3 is not simply due to differences in average skill levels between men and women.

25. The thirty-seven cultures are: Nigeria, South Africa (whites), South Africa (Zulu), Zambia, China, India, Indonesia, Iran, Israel (Jewish), Israel (Palestine), Japan, Taiwan, Bulgaria, Estonia, Poland, Yugoslavia, Belgium, France, Finland, West Germany, Great Britain, Greece, Ireland, Italy, Netherlands, Norway, Spain, Sweden, Canada (English), Canada (French), United States (mainland), United States (Hawaii), Australia, New Zealand, Brazil, Colombia, Venezuela.

26. Although this is an invaluable data source, there are other limitations of the data. The samples are not representative of the populations in each country, and rural, less-educated, and lower-income areas in particular are underrepresented. Furthermore, sampling techniques varied widely across countries. In some countries only high school students were interviewed; in another, surveys were taken of couples applying for marriage licenses; and in another, respondents were gleaned from newspaper advertisements.

27. Note that although the dependent variable can take on only four values, the regression is on country averages, which is a continuous variable. The variable is bound by 0 and 3, but nonlinear estimations do not improve the fit.

28. The total estimated changes in values as a result of changes in the employment structure correspond to roughly one interquartile difference on each of the preference variables in the cross-sectional data (see the "box and whisker" plots on the right in figure 2.8). This adds to the recent literature on deindustrialization, which argues that the rise of services has transformed the welfare state and redistributive politics (Esping-Andersen 1990; Iversen and Wren 1998; Iversen and Cusack 2000) and led to a rising gender gap in social policy preferences (Iversen and Rosenbluth 2006).

29. Since the United States is an early industrializer, with only 18 percent of the labor force in agricultural employment by 1939, employment in industry and services are almost perfectly negatively correlated ($r = -.85$). We can therefore use service employment as a good proxy for the employment structure in this period, and it turns out to be strongly positively correlated with the dependent variables ($r = .8, .6,$ and $.9$, re-

spectively). Of course, we cannot exclude other causes given the small *N*, but the combination of evidence tells a story that is very supportive of the view that gender norms change with the relative economic mobility of men and women, which is in turn determined by the skills required to participate effectively in the economy.

Chapter 3. The Gender Division of Labor, or Why Women Work Double Shifts

1. Gary Becker's pioneering work opened the economics of the family as a new field of study for economists. Becker 1964, 1971, 1981, 1985.

2. In treating marriage as an incomplete contract, we build on recent economic bargaining models of the family including Folbre 1987; Braunstein and Folbre 2001; Pollak 1999, 2003; Lundberg and Pollak 1996, 2001.

3. See Hall and Soskice 2001; Iversen, Pontusson, and Soskice 2000.

4. Esping-Andersen 1990, 1999; Orloff 1993; Huber and Stephens 2001.

5. Although the gains from trade are within the family, the model is exactly parallel to the argument David Ricardo made in the nineteenth century for why Britain would gain from removing restrictions on trade with the outside world. Britain would specialize in the production of goods in which it had a comparative rather than an absolute advantage.

6. Becker 1981.

7. Hrdy 1999.

8. Polachek 1975, 1978.

9. Lundberg and Pollak 1996.

10. Braunstein and Folbre 2001; Lundberg and Pollak 1996, 2001; Rosenbluth, Light, and Schrag 2004.

11. For a formal proof of this using a standard bargaining model, see Iversen, Rosenbluth, and Soskice 2005.

12. At the other extreme, if the returns to specialization in family work exist but are hard to observe, or are not sufficiently internalized by either parent, we might expect suboptimal levels of child welfare to result from a decline in specialization. We are assuming, though perhaps without justification, that both parents have a full and equal interest in their children's well being, so that their bargaining over paid and unpaid work does not include the possibility of a lower overall level of investment in their children.

13. Mincer 1962, 1978; Polachek 1975, 1978.

14. Anderson, Binder, and Krause 2002.

15. Estévez-Abe (1999) and Estévez-Abe et al. (2001).

16. Estévez-Abe 2002.

17. Hall and Soskice 2001; Iversen 2005.

18. The exception is Scandinavia where part-time workers are also highly unionized and where frequent center-left governments have given them a voice in public policies.

19. Orloff 1993; Esping-Andersen 1999.

20. The data for our analysis are from the 1994 International Social Survey Pro-

gramme, which focuses on the family and gender relations. The data cover most established democracies, a few East European transition economies, and one developing
country (the Philippines). We focus on the former since we have macrolevel data for
our institutional and labor market variables for these countries. None of these data are
available for the East European cases, which transitioned to democracy a few years before the survey and were still in the early phase of privatization. The cases included in
the analysis below are Australia, Austria, Canada, Ireland, Italy, (West) Germany,
Japan, the Netherlands, New Zealand, Norway, Spain, Sweden, the United Kingdom,
and the United States. One case, Spain, is missing so many of the key independent
variables that it had to be excluded from the individual-level analysis (but we kept it in
the macrolevel analysis).

21. Hochschild and Machung 1989.

22. The complete factor loadings are as follows:

	Factor 1	Factor 2
Laundry	0.51	−0.09
Caring for sick	0.59	0.08
Shopping	0.67	0.01
Dinner	0.66	−0.05
Repairs	0.15	0.22

23. Bittman et al. 2001. Time diaries, which ask respondents to keep track of how
they allocate time during the day, are preferable to less complete surveys of this sort.
Unfortunately, they are available for only a few countries.

24. Berthoud and Gershuny 2000.

25. Since we have information only about the income of the respondent, the earnings of the spouse are inferred from information about household income. To do this
we have to assume that all income is wage income and that husband and wife are the
only wage earners in the household. Since there are non-wage sources of income, and
sometimes more than two adult wage earners, this would suggest that income estimates based on the difference between family income and the respondent's income
exceed the latter on average. In fact, inferred incomes of spouses are slightly lower
than respondent incomes but generally very similar (within 90 percent of the respondent's income). This suggests that the inferred number is a fairly good proxy for the
spouse's income. It does at any rate not *systematically* bias the estimates of male and
female income since the respondents were roughly equally divided between men and
women.

26. There is no direct measure of the probability of divorce at the individual level,
so we use past divorce as a (very imperfect) proxy since we know that the aggregate
likelihood of divorce is higher for those who are previously divorced (Bramlett and
Mosher 2002). The variable is coded 1 if one of the spouses is previously divorced, 0
otherwise.

27. We capture this logic using a battery of questions about past family-related labor
market absences. Specifically, the questions inquire about time taken off during four
different phases of child rearing: (1) before the birth of the first child, (2) before the

youngest child entered school, (3) after the youngest child entered school, and (4) after the children have left home. The variable takes on the value 1 when the wo(man) did not work during any of these periods, and the value 0 when the wo(man) worked full time during all four periods (part-time work is coded .5). This coding follows Librizzi (2003).

28. The number of dependents is calculated by combining information about the number of household members with information about whether the family is headed by one or two adults. In most cases it refers to the number of children, although it will also capture older generations of family members living in the household.

29. The variable is measured in terms of seven levels of general education ranging from none (1) to a completed university degree (7).

30. Following Barro and McCleary (2003), we measure religiosity by frequency of church attendance, which varies from never to at least once a week. Catholicism is measured using the respondent's declared religion.

31. The number of part-time employees is from the OECD online Labour Force Statistics Database (www.oecd.org/scripts/cde/members/LFSDATAAuthenticate .asp), and the working-age population is the number of people between the ages of eighteen and sixty-five, obtained from the OECD (OECD, *Labour Force Statistics,* 2003).

32. Because both workers and employers want to reap the long-term benefits of specific skills investments, and because workers with such skills will find it harder to move around, firm tenure rates tend to be longer for workers with highly specific skills. This is an imperfect measure of skill specificity, however, because skills may be specific to an industry or occupation, which allows workers to move around between firms in the same industry or occupation. This problem is avoided by focusing on vocational training intensity. Such training is intended to provide skills that are much more specific to particular jobs than those acquired through general education, but it includes training in skills that are specific to industries or occupations, not just particular firms. Indeed the drawback of using vocational training intensity as a measure is that it does not fully capture training at the firm level. As argued in Estévez-Abe, Iversen, and Soskice (2001) and Iversen (2005), the two measures therefore complement each other, compensating for weaknesses in each. In combination they provide a good summary measure of differences in national training systems described by detailed case studies. Vocational training intensity is the share of an age cohort in either secondary or post-secondary (ISCED5) vocational training. Source: UNESCO 1999.Tenure rates are the median length of enterprise tenure in years (Norwegian figure refers to 1991). Sources: *OECD Employment Outlook,* 1997, table 5.5. For Norway: *OECD Employment Outlook,* 1993, table 4.1.

33. The public consumption data are from OECD, *National Accounts, Part II: Detailed Tables* (Paris: OECD, various years), and the military spending data are from the International Institute for Peace and Conflict Research, 1995.

34. Note that in this case the dependent variable is the division of labor, not the total amount of labor. So even though the state may remove caring responsibilities from

the family, this does not affect the division of the remaining labor except through its effect on bargaining (hours of work are also controlled for).

35. Pooling data across levels without taking into account the dependence of observations within clusters carries a significant risk that standard errors will be underestimated and that estimated parameter biased (Burton, Gurrin, and Sly 1998; Steenbergen and Jones 2002).

36. It is true that in the efficiency model as the earnings capacity of the woman increases, some low-productivity activities (such as housekeeping) may be subcontracted out. But our analysis concerns the division of labor that is actually performed by the spouses, which should be complete in the efficiency model.

37. Granted, the appropriate measure in the efficiency model is not total income but productivity or hourly income at equivalent hours of work. It seems unlikely, though, that this alternative measure would much affect the results.

38. The two subsample results suggest that age *reduces* household labor for men, but since the ages of the cohabiting couple are highly collinear we do not know if this is because the female spouse is getting older.

39. Twenty years in age is equal to .12 units on the dependent variable, and a unit is equivalent to about 115 minutes of work.

40. Multiply the age parameter for paid work in table 3.2 by the parameter for paid work in the household regression in table 3.1 and compare it to the parameter for age in that regression. The indirect negative effect of age turns out to be greater than the positive direct effect.

41. Lundberg and Pollak 1996, 2001; Braunstein and Folbre 2001.

Chapter 4. Fertility

1. Logically, investment in firm-specific skills may be firms' response to politically mandated long-term labor contracts, or the preference for long-term contracts can reflect firms' commitment to incremental production methods. The varieties of capitalism literature has taken the latter position, but it is an empirical question that is beyond the scope of this book to explore. Suffice it now to say that the former argument implies that partisan commitments protect specific skills jobs beyond their economic value, whereas the latter predicts a shift toward shorter labor contracts with the rise of the service sector.

2. The price level is measured as the log of the inverse of the real exchange rate, using the U.S. dollar as the reference currency, *minus* the effect of GDP/capita on the real exchange rate (because prices are a positive function of development). Positive values imply higher prices on nontraded goods relative to the U.S. dollar. Because prices do not differ much on traded goods, they are largely a measure of the prices on services.

3. The Danish government, for example, has spent enormous sums relocating workers from uncompetitive meat packing plants and such to a whole range of service sector jobs.

4. Pooling data across levels requires that we take into account the dependence of

observations within clusters. We therefore use the multilevel modeling approach, which is explained in detail in appendix A for chapter 3. The general setup is

$$(1)\ y_{ij} = \beta_{0j} + \sum_{r=1}^{R} \beta_{rj} x_{rij} + \sum_{s=1}^{S} \phi_{0s} z_{sj} + \varepsilon_{ij}.$$

where y is the dependent variable (fertility), x_r are individual-level explanatory variables (indexed by r), and z_s are country-level predictors (indexed by s). Individuals are indexed by i, and countries by j. We will also test cross-level interactions ($x \times z$), but we can ignore these for now. Our multilevel results are complemented by macrolevel regressions for a larger sample of countries and years.

5. The countries are Australia, Canada, Denmark, Finland, Italy, Japan, Portugal, and New Zealand in addition to the countries included in the microsamples (excluding Greece).

6. In the cases of Finland and Switzerland this information is not available. Instead, we used the number of persons in the household, minus 1 for singles or divorced and minus 2 for married couples. The resulting variable is correlated with the number of children in the household (among countries where both variables are available).

7. Sector of employment is recorded only for people currently in employment, which means that those women who have temporarily exited the labor market for family reasons are excluded. These women are likely to come disproportionately from flexible types of employment, which will cause the effects of sector and occupation to be underestimated. But any bias will weigh against our hypotheses.

8. Because long educations increase the time it takes to establish a career, and therefore tend to reduce fertility, skill specificity is not here measured relatively to total skills as is in Iversen and Soskice (2001).

9. Specifically, vocational training intensity is the share of an age cohort in either secondary or postsecondary (ISCED5) vocational training. Source: UNESCO 1999. Tenure rates are the median length of enterprise tenure in years, Norwegian figure refers to 1991). Sources: *OECD Employment Outlook*, 1997, table 5.5. For Norway: *OECD Employment Outlook*, 1993, table 4.1.

10. Estévez-Abe et al. 2001; Iversen 2005.

11. We measure both effects of public sector by calculating government spending on goods and services (excluding defense), as a share of GDP. In practice, the bulk of nonmilitary government purchases are for social services that are either (in large measure) provided *by* women or *for* women. The public consumption data are from OECD, *National Accounts, Part II: Detailed Tables* (Paris: OECD, various years), and the military spending data are from the Stockholm International Peace Research Institute, *World Armaments and Disarmament: SIPRI Yearbook*, 1995.

12. Esping-Andersen, of course, pointed this out long ago (1990, 1999).

13. Since the macrodata are pooled cross section time series these results correct for first-order serial correlation and contemporaneous correlation using Prais Winsten estimates with panel-corrected standard errors (Beck and Katz 1995).

14. Goldin 1990.

15. Blau and Kahn 2005; Goldin 1990; O'Neill and Polacheck 1993; Brinton 2007.

16. Brinton 2007.

17. Brinton 1993, 2007.

18. Brinton 2007.

19. Blau and Kahn 1996.

20. Huber and Stephens 2000.

21. Because Japan does not participate in the Luxembourg Income Survey, data on fertility by income are not available for Japan.

22. Kenjoh 2005.

23. Gustafsson, Kenjoh, and Wetzels 2001.

24. Scharpf 2000.

25. Uwe Becker 2005.

Chapter 5. Political Preferences

1. The formation of public policy preferences from underlying economic interests is assumed in political economy models, but how individuals come to understand how policy affects interests is itself subject to explanation. Iversen and Soskice (2009) underscore the role of social networks and incentives, but it is not an idea we are able to test empirically with our data. The difficulty of translating new economic conditions into policy preferences is one reason that social norms take time to change and, in our view, often occurs only through intergenerational change. This is an important area of future research.

2. Mincer 1958, 1978; Polachek 1975, 1981.

3. Anderson, Binder, and Krause 2003.

4. Estévez-Abe 1999 and Estévez-Abe et al. 2001.

5. Hall and Soskice 2001; Iversen 2005.

6. Institutions that protect private sector specific skills, such as high job security, seniority pay, and generous employer-financed benefits, tend to reinforce insider-outsider divisions, and since women are more likely to be outsiders, they are at a greater disadvantage compared to more flexible labor markets where low protection encourages investment in general skills.

7. Esping-Andersen 1999; Orloff 1999.

8. Note that the private sector in Scandinavia is a characteristically specific skills economy. One can view the large services component of the public sector counteracting the effects of the private sector specific skills economy, or as pulling the Scandinavian economies into a general skills direction. Although they are analytically equivalent, we adopt the former approach only for ease of presentation.

9. Lott and Kenny 1999.

10. Inglehart and Norris 2000, 20003; Studlar, McAllister, and Hayes 1998.

11. Blaydes and Linzer 2008; Ross 2008.

12. Kaufmann 2002; Kaufmann and Petrocik 1999; Box-Steffenmeier, De Boef, and Lin 2004; Chaney, Alvarzz, and Nagler 1998; Miller 1999; Iversen and Rosenbluth, 2006; Iversen, Rosenbluth, and Soskice 2005.

13. Alvarez and McCaffery 2000; Greenberg 2000; Ladd 1997; Shapiro and Mahajan 1986. Sanbonmatsu (2002, 2006) finds that voters expect female candidates to be more welfarist as well.

14. Conover 1988; Welch and Hibbing 1992; Gidengil 1995.

15. Tedin 1994; Sears and Citrin 1982.

16. Goertzel 1983; Carroll 1988; Inglehart and Norris 2000, 2003.

17. Edlund and Pande 2002.

18. Greenberg 2000

19. One could argue, of course, that there is a selection effect here: only the women who feel at the greatest risk will seek outside employment, since their resulting outside remuneration partially offsets their perceived risk.

20. One could also focus on declared voting choices, but expressed support for a party arguably captures a more stable underlying preference that *is* not affected by short-term political issues for which we have no measures.

21. The data are from "Society at a Glance: OECD Social Indicators," OECD 2001.

22. The variable is adopted from Iversen and Soskice 2001.

23. The results for left partisanship are based on binomial logistic regression.

24. This also implies that the effect of gender goes through, although it is slightly weakened, if we exclude the two Scandinavian countries that are known to have large gender gaps (Svallfors 1997). Specifically the coefficient on the gender (female) variable drops from 0.176 to 0.146 (both significant at the .01 level).

25. Roemer 1998.

26. In the Steenbergen and Jones (2002) setup explained in the appendix to chapter 3, the variation in some individual-level parameters, indexed by q, can be modeled as a function of R national-level variables, $z_{rq} : \beta_{qj} = \gamma_{q0} + \sum_{r=1}^{R} \gamma_{qr} z_{rj} + \delta_{qj}$.

27. We cannot show results for "level" in the case of preferences because differences across countries are absorbed by the country dummies.

28. This is specifically true in West Bengal, where drinking water and roads are higher priorities for women than for men. In Rajasthan, where women are less concerned about roads, female representation is not correlated to road investment. Chattopadhyay and Duflo 2004, 1411ff.

Chapter 6. Gender and Political Careers

1. Carey and Shugart 1995.

2. The only other potential concern of the leadership in this game will be that enough potential future leaders are recruited to maintain the party's image among voters as competent. But this requires farsightedness, and it may easily be outweighed by concerns about recruiting overly ambitious candidates who might challenge their own leadership.

3. Estévez-Abe et al. 2001; Estévez-Abe 2007.

4. Persson and Tabellini 2005.

5. Estévez-Abe 1999; Iversen and Rosenbluth 2006.

6. Cusack, Iversen, and Soskice (2007) provide an account of the historical origins of the linkage between PR and organized capitalism.

7. We also tried an alternative model specification where a lagged dependent variable is used to remove first-order serial correlation (shown in column 2 of table 6.4).

In this formulation the predicted long-run effects of a 1 percent change in the female share of the labor force and a 1 percent increase in service sector employment are to raise female representation by.78 and 1 percent. The average changes in female employment and service employment between the 1960s and 2000 now translate into a 26 percent increase in representation, which is "too large" compared to the actually observed change of 18 percent. A well-known source of this problem is that the lagged dependent variable can bias the results if it captures effects other than first-order serial correlation (which arises in our data primarily because incumbents are slow to be replaced). The Prais Winsten regression avoids this problem.

8. For the other results reported in figure 6.2 we have substituted GDP per capita for service employment because we have data for all twenty-three countries on the former variable, but only for twenty-one countries on the latter. The correlation between the two variables is high (.77), and none of the results are notably affected by using GDP per capita instead of service employment. The long-run predictions are also very similar (see column 3 in table 6.4 for details). To maximize country coverage, and since we are primarily interested in the effects of political institutions, we therefore use GDP per capita in the rest of the analysis.

9. Carey and Shugart (1995) developed a ranking of countries according to their assessment of the effects of a variety of electoral system attributes on the incentives of candidates to cultivate a personal vote. Their ranking is obviously relevant to our explanation, but it is based on a large number of (implicit) discretionary decisions about the importance of different variables, which can be contested. We prefer to keep the salient dimensions of the electoral system separate and let the data speak about salience. In the end, the composite variable we construct below is correlated with their ranking at a .85 level. We should also note that we are not directly using two of Carey and Shugart's variables: one they call "vote" that refers to "whether voters cast a single intra-party vote instead of multiple votes or a party-level vote," and one they call "ballot" that refers to whether parties control candidate access and position on a party list. There is practically no variance on the former variable in our sample. We discuss the relationship between the variables we use and the ballot or list variable below.

10. This follows Carey and Shugart (1995) and the implementation of their coding scheme by Johnson and Wallack (2007).

11. The pooling variable in our sample of countries is almost identical to distinguishing between list and other types of electoral systems (a distinction we used in the theoretical discussion and is captured by what Carey and Shugart in their coding scheme refer to as "ballot"). Where there is no pooling, there is typically no party list. The sole exception is Japan before the electoral reforms in 1994. Here parties made up lists of candidates, but votes for each candidate were not transferable to other candidates (i.e., no pooling). As a result, candidates from the same party had a strong incentive to differentiate themselves from each other, and a vote for any candidate was not primarily a vote for the party platform. For our purposes the incentives to cultivate a personal following in the SNTV system is captured by the pooling variable, not by a variable distinguishing between lists and no lists. There is also an exception to the rule that no-list systems do not use pooling: Luxembourg. In this system candidates run on

party platforms, but parties do not make up their own lists. But since votes are pooled for each party, voters cannot ignore party platforms and the system in effect works very much like a typical European list system. The key for our purposes is therefore again the pooling. Excluding Japan and Luxembourg, the correlation between pooling variable and a list variable is .89, and it is perfect ($r = 1$) if the ambiguous cases between 0 and 1 on the pooling variable are omitted.

12. The latter variable is from the Cusack and Engelhart (2002) data set on political parties.

13. We use a methodology proposed by Blanchard and Wolfers (1999).

14. The female candidates who *are* nominated for district-level seats are likely to be equally competitive with men. They are simply fewer. This follows from the assumption that parties are trying win elections.

15. We assume here a principal-agent model of political parties, in which back-benchers delegate authority to the front bench depending on how well their individual electoral chances are served by strengthening party coherence and discipline.

16. For ease of interpretation, the lowest value for the female share of the labor force variable has been set to 0. This means that the effect of the list variable when the female labor force share is at its minimum is simply the parameter on the list variable.

17. Uhlaner and Lehman Schlozman 1986; Cox 2000; Sanbonmatsu 2002, 2006.

18. Our argument is similar to Uhlaner's and Lehman-Schlozman's, who found that females tend to raise less campaign money because they are more likely to be running as challengers rather than as incumbents. "Donors behaved like bookmakers—what mattered was which horse would cross the finish line first, not whether it was a filly or a colt" (Uhlaner and Lehman-Schlozman 1986, 43). Gaddie and Bullock (1997) and Smith and Fox (2001) found that female candidates do well in open seat elections that they contest. But we note that females do not put themselves forward for open seat elections in numbers equal to male candidates, and we attribute this reticence to the importance of district-specific investments in the U.S. system, in which male candidates have a decisive advantage.

19. "Accounts of Feminism among Women Local Councillors in England," *Women's Studies International Forum* 26 (4): 345.

20. See http://www.scb.se/templates/Product___12337.asp, and "Local Government Sweden Fact Sheet," http://www.sweden.se/upload/Sweden_se/english/factsheets/SI/SI_FS527_Local Government_in_Sweden/FS52vLowres.pdf.

Chapter 7. Conclusions

1. David Hume; Lewis 1969; Chwe 2001. But these posit, rather than establish, the cognitive processes involved.

2. These questions are at the heart of the debate about descriptive representation as a remedy to the insufficiency of substantive representation. Squires 1996; Rehfeld 2006; Mansbridge and Moller Okin 2007.

3. See Iversen and Soskice (2008) for a formal exposition of the logic.

REFERENCES

Alvarez, R. Michael, and Edward McCaffery. 2000. "Is There a Gender Gap in Fiscal Political Preferences?" Paper presented at the annual meeting of the American Political Science Association.

Anderson, Deborah, Melissa Binder, and Kate Krause. 2002. "The Motherhood Wage Penalty: Which Mothers Pay It and Why?" *American Economic Review Papers and Proceedings* 92 (2): 354–58.

———. 2003. "The Motherhood Gap Revisited: Experience, Heterogeneity, Work Effort and Work-Schedule Flexibility," *Industrial and Labor Relations Review* 56 (2): 273–94.

Baker, Matthew, and Joyce Jacobsen. 2007. "Marriage, Specialization, and the Gender Division of Labor." *Journal of Labor Economics* 25 (4): 763–94.

Barro, Robert J., and Rachel M. McCleary. 2003. "Religion and Economic Growth." NBER Working Paper Series: 9682. National Bureau of Economic Research, Inc. http://www.nber.org/papers/w9682.

Beck, Nathaniel, and Jonathan Katz. 1995. "What to Do (and Not to Do) with Time-Series Cross-Section Data." *American Political Science Review* 89 no. 3 (September): 634–47.

Becker, Gary. 1964. *Human Capital*. New York: Columbia University Press.

———. 1965. "A Theory of the Allocation of Time." *Economic Journal* 75 (299): 493–517.

———. 1971. *The Economics of Discrimination*. Chicago: University of Chicago Press.

———. 1981. *A Treatise on the Family*. Cambridge: Harvard University Press.

———. 1985. "Human Capital, Effort, and the Sexual Division of Labor." *Journal of Labor Economics* 3 (1/2): S33–S58.

Becker, Uwe. 2005. "An Example of Competitive Corporatism? The Dutch Political Economy 1983–2004 in Critical Examination." *Journal of European Public Policy* 12 (6): 1078–1102.

Berthoud, Richard, and Jonathan Gershuny, eds. 2000. *Seven Years in the Lives of*

British Families: Evidence on the Dynamics of Social Change from the British House-hold Panel Survey. Bristol: Policy Press.

Bittman, Michael, Paula England, Nancy Folbre, and George Matheson. 2001. "When Gender Trumps Money: Bargaining and Time in Household Work." JCPR Working Papers 221, Northwestern University/University of Chicago Joint Center for Poverty Research.

Blanchard, Olivier, and Justin Wolfers. 1999. "The Role of Shocks and Institutions in the Rise of European Unemployment: The Aggregate Evidence." NBER Working Paper Series: 7282. National Bureau of Economic Research, Inc. http://www.nber .org/papers/w7282.

Blau, Francine D., and Lawrence M. Kahn, 1996. "The Gender Earning Gap: Some International Evidence." NBER Working Paper Series: 4224. National Bureau of Economic Research, Inc. http://ideas.repec.org/s/nbr/nberwo.html.

———. 2007. "Changes in the Labor Supply Behavior of Married Women, 1980–2000." *Journal of Labor Economics* 25:393–438.

Blaydes, Lisa, and Drew Linzer. 2008. "The Political Economy of Women's Support for Fundamentalist Islam." *World Politics* 60 (4): 576–609.

Blumberg, Rae Lesser. 1984. "A General Theory of Gender Stratification." *Sociological Theory* 2:23–101.

———. 2004. "Extending Lenski's Schema to Hold Up Both Halves of the Sky: A Theory Guided Way of Conceptualizing Agrarian Societies that Illuminates a Puzzle about Gender Stratification." *Sociological Theory* 22 (2): 278–291.

Bowlby, John. 1951. *Maternal Care and Mental Health.* New York: Schocken.

———. 1990. *A Secure Base: Parent-Child Attachment and Healthy Human Development.* New York: Basic Books.

Box-Steffensmeier, Janet, Suzanna De Boef, and Tse Min Lin. 2004. "The Dynamics of the Partisan Gender Gap." *American Political Science Review* 98:515–25.

Bradshaw, Jonathan. 2005. "Child Benefit Packages in 22 Countries." Research Report No. 174. Social Policy Research Unit, University of York.

Bramlett, M. D., and W. D. Mosher. 2002. "Cohabitation, Marriage, Divorce, and Remarriage in the United States." National Center for Health Statistics, *Vital Health Stat,* 23:22.

Braunstein, Elissa, and Nancy Folbre. 2001. "To Honor and Obey: Efficiency, Inequality, and Patriarchal Property Rights." *Feminist Economics* 7 (1): 25–44.

Brinton, Mary. 1993. *Women and the Economic Miracle: Gender and Work in Postwar Japan.* Berkeley: University of California Press.

———. 2007. "Gendered Offices: A Comparative-Historical Examination of Clerical Work in Japan and the U.S." In *The Political Economy of Low Fertility: Japan in Comparative Perspective,* ed. Frances McCall Rosenbluth. Stanford: Stanford University Press.

Burgoon, Brian, and Michael Hiscox. 2004. "The Mysterious Case of Female Protectionism: Gender Bias in the Attitudes and Politics of International Trade." Paper presented at the annual meeting of the American Political Science Association, Chicago.

Burton, P. R., L. C. Gurrin, and M. J. Campbell. 1998. "Clinical Significance Not Statistical Significance: A Simple Bayesian Alternative to p Values." *Journal of Epidemiology and Community Health* 52:318–23.

Burton, P., L. Gurrin, and P. Sly. 1998. "Extending the Simple Linear Regression Model for Correlated Responses: An Introduction to Generalized Estimating Equations and Multi-Level Mixed Modeling." *Statistics in Medicine* 17: 1261–91.

Buss, D. M. 1989. "Sex Differences in Human Mate Preferences: Evolutionary Hypotheses Tested in 37 Cultures." *Behavioral and Brain Sciences* 12:1–49.

Buss, D. M., T. K. Shackelford, L. A. Kirkpatrick, and R. J. Larsen. 2001. "A Half Century of American Mate Preferences: The Cultural Evolution of Values." *Journal of Marriage and the Family* 63:491–503.

Carey, J., and M. Shugart. 1995. "Incentives to Cultivate a Personal Vote: A Rank Ordering of Electoral Formulas." *Electoral Studies* 14:417–39.

Carroll, Susan. 1988. "Women's Autonomy and the Gender Gap: 1980 and 1982." In *The Politics of the Gender Gap: The Social Construction of Political Influence,* ed. Carol Mueller. London: Sage Press.

Chaney, Carole, Michael Alvarez, and Jonathan Nagler. 1998. "Explaining the Gender Gap in the U.S. Presidential Elections, 1980–1992." *Political Research Quarterly* 51:311–40.

Chattopadhyay, Raghabendra, and Esther Duflo. 2004. "Woman as Policy Makers: Evidence from a Randomized Policy Experiment in India." *Econometrica* 72 (5): 1409–43.

Chwe, Michael Suk-Young. 2001. *Rational Ritual Culture, Coordination and Common Knowledge.* Princeton: Princeton University Press.

Collins, Randall. 1971. "A Conflict Theory of Sexual Stratification." *Social Problems* 19:3–21.

Collins, Randall, Janet Saltzman Chafetz, Rae Lesser Blumberg, Scott Coltrane, and Jonathan H. Turner. 1993. "Toward an Integrated Theory of Gender Stratification." *Sociological Perspectives* 36 (3): 185–216.

Conover, Pamela Johnston. 1988. "Feminists and the Gender Gap." *Journal of Politics* 50 (4): 985–1010.

Cox, Gary W. 2000. "On the Effects of Legislative Rules." *Legislative Studies Quarterly* 25:169–92.

Cusack T., and L. Englehart. 2002. *The PGL File Collection.* Berlin: Wiss. Berlin Sozialforschung.

Cusack, Thomas R., Torben Iversen, and Philipp Rehm. 2006. "Risks at Work: The Demand and Supply Sides of Government Redistribution." *Oxford Review of Economic Policy* 22 (3): 365–89.

Cusack, Thomas R., Torben Iversen, and David Soskice. 2007. "Economic Interests and the Origins of Electoral Systems." *American Political Science Review* 10 (3): 373–91.

Dahlberg, Frances, ed. 1981. *Woman the Gatherer.* New Haven: Yale University Press.

Divale, Robert, and Marvin Harris. 1976. "Population, Warfare, and the Male Supremacist Complex." *American Anthropologist* 78:521–38.

Du, Shanshan. 2006. *"Chopsticks Only Work in Pairs": Gender Unity and Gender Equality among the Lahu of Southwest China.* New York: Columbia University Press.

Edlund, Lena, and Rohini Pande. 2002. "Why Have Women Become Left-Wing? The Political Gender Gap and the Decline in Marriage." *Quarterly Journal of Economics* 117 (3): 917–61.

Engels, Friedrich. 1985 [1884]. *The Origin of the Family, Private Property and the State.* New York: Penguin Classics.

Esping-Andersen, Gosta. 1990. *The Three Worlds of Welfare Capitalism.* Princeton: Princeton University Press.

———. 1999. *Social Foundations of Postindustrial Economies.* New York: Oxford University Press.

Estévez-Abe, Margarita. 1999. "Multiple Logics of the Welfare State: Skills, Protection and Female Labor in Japan and Selected OECD Countries." U.S.–Japan Program Working Paper 99–02, Harvard University.

———. 2002. "Negotiating Welfare Reforms: Actors and Institutions in the Japanese Welfare State." In *Restructuring the Welfare State: Political Institutions and Policy Change,* ed. Sven Steinmo and Bo Rothstein. New York: Palgrave Macmillan.

———. 2007. "Gendering the Varieties of Capitalism: Gender Bias in Skills and Social Policy." In *The Political Economy of Japan's Low Fertility,* ed. Frances Rosenbluth. Stanford: Stanford University Press.

Estévez-Abe M., T. Iversen, and D. Soskice. 2001. "Social Protection and the Formation of Skills: A Reinterpretation of the Welfare State." In *Varieties of Capitalism: The Institutional Foundations of Comparative Advantage,* ed. P. Hall and D. Soskice. New York: Oxford University Press.

Folbre, Nancy. 1987. *Field Guide to the U.S. Economy.* New York: Pantheon Books.

Gaddie, R. K., and C. S. Bullock III. 1997. "Structural and Elite Features in Open Seat and Special U.S. House Elections: Is There a Sexual Bias?" *Political Research Quarterly* 50:459–68.

Geddes, Rick, and Dean Lueck. 2002. "The Gains from Self-Ownership and the Expansion of Women's Rights." *American Economic Review* 92 (4): 1079–92.

Gidengil, Elisabeth. 1995. "Economic Man, Social Woman: The Case of the Gender Gap in Support of the Canada–United States Free-Trade Agreement." *Comparative Political Studies* 23 (3): 384–408.

Gilman, Charlotte Perkins. 1898. *Women and Economics.* Boston: Small, Maynard. Repr. London: Dover Publications, 1998.

Goertzel, Ted George. 1983. "The Gender Gap: Sex, Family Income, and Political Opinions in the Early 1980s." *Journal of Political and Military Sociology* 11:209–22.

Goldin, Claudia. 1990. *Understanding the Gender Gap: An Economic History of American Women.* New York: Oxford University Press.

———. 1991. "The Role of World War II in the Rise of Women's Employment." *American Economic Review* 81 (4): 741–56.

Greenberg, Anna. 2000. "Deconstructing the Gender Gap." Working Paper, John F. Kennedy School of Government, Harvard University.

Gustafsson, Siv S., Eiko Kenjoh, and Cécile Wetzels. 2001. "Does Part-Time and Intermittent Work during Early Motherhood Lead to Regular Work Later? A Comparison of Labor Behavior of Mothers with Young Children in Germany, Britain, the Netherlands and Sweden." *Vierteljahrshefte zur Wirtschaftsforschung/Quarterly Journal of Economic Research*, DIW Berlin, German Institute for Economic Research, 70 (1): 15–23.

Hall, Peter, and David Soskice, eds. 2001. *Varieties of Capitalism: The Institutional Foundations of Comparative Advantage.* New York: Oxford University Press.

Harris, Judith Rich. 1998. *The Nurture Assumption: Why Children Turn Out the Way They Do.* New York: Free Press.

Hawkes, Kristen. 1981. "A Third Explanation for Female Infanticide." *Human Ecology* 9 (1): 76–96.

———. 1993. "Why Hunter-Gatherers Work: An Ancient Version of the Problem of Public Goods." *Current Anthropology* 34:341–61.

Hill, Kim, and A. Magdalena Hurtado. 1997. "The Evolution of Premature Reproductive Senescence and Menopause in Human Females: An Evaluation of the 'Grandmother Hypothesis.'" In *Human Nature: A Critical Reader,* ed. Laura Betzig, 118–139. New York: Oxford University Press.

Hochschild, A., and A. Machung. 1989. *The Second Shift: Working Parents and the Revolution at Home.* New York: Viking Adult.

Hrdy, Sarah Blaffer. 1981. *The Woman That Never Evolved.* Cambridge: Harvard University Press.

———. 1999. *Mother Nature.* New York: Norton.

Huber, Evelyn, and John D. Stephens. 2000. "Partisan Governance, Women's Employment, and the Social Democratic Service State." *American Sociological Review* 65 (3): 323–42.

———. 2001. *Development and Crisis of the Welfare State: Parties and Policies in Global Markets,* Chicago: Chicago University Press.

Inglehart, Ronald, and Pippa Norris. 2000. "The Developmental Theory of the Gender Gap: Women and Men's Voting Behavior in Global Perspective." *International Political Science Review* 21 (4): 441–463.

———. 2003. "The Gender Gap in Voting and Public Opinion." In *Rising Tide: Gender Equality and Cultural Change around the World.* Cambridge: Cambridge University Press.

International Labor Organization, "Labor Statistics Database." ILO, 1998–2004.

International Social Survey Program (ISSP). 1994. International Social Survey Program: Family and Changing Gender Roles II. http://dx.doi.org/10.3886/ICPSR 06914.

Iversen, Torben. 2005. *Capitalism, Democracy, and Welfare.* New York: Cambridge University Press.

Iversen, Torben, and Thomas Cusack. 2000. "The Causes of Welfare Expansion: Deindustrialization or Globalization?" *World Politics* 52 (3): 313–49.

Iverson, Torben, Jomas Pontusson, and David Soskice. 2000. *Unions, Employers, and Central Banks: Macroeconomic Coordination and Institutional Change in Social Market Economies.* New York: Cambridge University Press.

Iversen, Torben, and Frances Rosenbluth. 2006. "The Political Economy of Gender: Explaining Cross-National Variation in Household Bargaining, Divorce, and the Gender Voting Gap." *American Journal of Political Science* 50 (1): 1–19.

Iversen, Torben, Frances Rosenbluth, and David Soskice. 2005. "Divorce and the Gender Division of Labor in Comparative Perspective." *Social Politics* 12 (2): 216–42.

Iversen, Torben, and David Soskice. 2001. "An Asset Theory of Social Policy Preferences." *American Political Science Review* 95 (4): 75–93.

———. 2008. "Electoral Institutions and the Politics of Coalitions: Why Some Democracies Redistribute More Than Others." http://ssrn.com/abstract/=1159452.

———. 2009. "Distribution and Redistribution: The Shadow of the Nineteenth Century." *World Politics* 61 (3): 438–86.

Iversen, Torben, and Anne Wren. 1998. "Equality, Employment and Budgetary Restraint: The Trilemma of the Service Economy." *World Politics* 50 (4): 507–46.

Johnson, Allan. 1997. *The Gender Knot: Unraveling Our Patriarchal Legacy.* Philadelphia: Temple University Press.

Johnson, J. W., and J. S. Wallack. 2007. *Electoral Systems and the Personal Vote.* http://dss.ucsd.edu/~jwjohnso/espv.htm.

Kaufmann, Karen. 2002. "Culture Wars, Secular Realignment and the Gender Gap in Party Identification." *Political Behavior* 24:283–307.

Kaufmann, Karen, and John Petrocik. 1999. "The Changing Politics of American Men: Understanding the Sources of the Gender Gap." *American Journal of Political Science* 43:864–87.

Kenjoh, Eiko. 2005. "New Mothers' Employment and Public Policy in the U.K., Germany, the Netherlands, Sweden and Japan." *LABOUR* 19 (1): 5–49.

Kenworthy, Lane. 2008. *Jobs with Equality.* New York: Oxford University Press.

Kenworthy, Lane, and Melissa Malami. 1999. "Gender Inequality in Political Representation: A Worldwide Comparative Analysis." *Social Forces* 78 (1): 235–69.

Keohane, Nannerl. 1980. *Philosophy and the State in France: The Renaissance to the Enlightenment.* Princeton: Princeton University Press.

Kuhn, S. L., and M. C. Stiner. 2001. "The Antiquity of Hunter-gatherers." In *Hunter-gatherers: Interdisciplinary Perspectives,* ed., C. Panter-Brick, R. H. Layton, and P. A. Rowley-Conwy. Cambridge: Cambridge University Press.

Ladd, Everett. 1997. "Framing the Gender Gap." In *Women, Media, and Politics,* ed. Pippa Norris. New York: Oxford University Press.

Leacock, Eleanor. 1978. "Women's Status in Egalitarian Society: Implications for Social Evolution." *Current Anthropology* 19 (2): 247–75.

Lee, Richard, and Irven Devore. 1999. *Man the Hunter.* Chicago: Aldine de Gruyter.

Lewis, David K. 1969. *Convention: A Philosophical Study.* Wiley-Blackwell.

Librizzi, Christopher J. 2003. "Bargaining and the Division of Household Labor: A Cross-National Analysis of Individual- and National-Level Factors." Honors thesis, Department of Government, Harvard College. "Local Government Sweden Fact

Sheet." http://www.sweden.se/upload/Sweden_se/english/factsheets/SI/SI_FS 527_LocalGovernment_in_Sweden/FS52vLowres.pdf.

Lott, John, and Lawrence Kenny. 1999. "Did Women's Suffrage Change the Size and Scope of Government?" *Journal of Political Economy* 107 (6): 1163–98.

Low, Bobbi. 2000. *Why Sex Matters: A Darwinian Look at Human Behavior.* Princeton: Princeton University Press.

Lundberg, Shelly, and Robert Pollack. 1996. "Bargaining and Distribution in Marriage." *Journal of Economic Perspectives* 10 (4): 139–58.

———. 2001. "Efficiency in Marriage." NBER Working Paper Series: 8642. National Bureau of Economic Research, Inc.

MacKinnon, Catharine. 1983. 'Feminism, Marxism, Method and the State: An Agenda for Theory.' *Signs: Journal of Women in Culture and Society* 515:7.

Mansbridge, Jane, and Susan Moller Okin. 2007. "Feminism." In *A Companion to Contemporary Political Theory,* 2nd ed., ed. Robert Goodin, Philip Pettit, and Thomas Pogge. London: Blackwell, 332–59.

McCloskey, Donald. 1993. "Some Consequences of a Conjective Economics." In *Beyond Economic Man: Feminist Theory and Economics,* ed. Marianne Ferber and Julie Nelson. Chicago: University of Chicago Press.

McCloskey, Deirdre, and Stephen Thomas Ziliak. 2003. *Measurement and Meaning in Economics: The Essential Deirdre McCloskey.* Cheltenham, U.K.: Edward Elgar Publishing.

McDonald, Peter. 2000. "Gender Equity, Social Institutions, and the Future of Fertility." *Journal of Population Research* 17 (1): 1–16.

McElroy, M., and M. Homey. 1981. "Nash-Bargained Household Decisions: Towards a Generalization of the Theory of Demand. *International Economic Review* 22 (2): 333–49.

Milkman, Ruth, Ellen Reese, and Benita Roth. 1998. "The Macrosociology of Paid Domestic Labor." *Work and Occupation* 25 (4): 483–510.

Miller, Warren. 1999. "Party Identification, Realignment and Party Voting: Back to Basics." *American Political Science Review* 85:557–68.

Mincer, Jacob. 1958. "Investment in Human Capital and Personal Income Distribution." *Journal of Political Economy* 66 (4): 281–302.

———. 1962. "On the Job Training: Costs, Returns, and Some Implications." *Journal of Political Economy* 70 (5): 50–79.

———. 1978. "Family Migration Decisions." *Journal of Political Economy* 86 (5): 749–73.

O'Connor, Julia, Ann Orloff, and Sheila Shaver. 1999. *States, Markets, Families: Gender, Liberalism and Social Policy in Australia, Canada, Great Britain, and the United States.* New York: Cambridge University Press.

O'Neill, June, and Solomon Polachek. 1993. "Why the Gender Gap in Wages Narrowed in the 1980s." *Journal of Labor Economics* 11 (1): 205–28.

OECD. 1993 and 1997. *OECD Employment Outlook.* Paris: OECD.

———. 2001. "Society at a Glance: OECD Social Indicators." Paris: OECD.

———. 2006. *Factbook 2006: Economic, Environmental and Social Statistics*. Paris: OECD.

———. Various years. *Labour Force Statistics*. "National Accounts, Part II: Detailed Tables." Paris: OECD.

Orloff, Ann Shola. 1993. "Gender and the Social Rights of Citizenship: The Comparative Analysis of Gender Relations and Welfare States." *American Sociological Review* 58:303–28.

———. 1999. "Motherhood, Work, and Welfare: Gender Ideologies and State Social Provision in Australia, Britain, Canada and the United States." In *State/Culture*, ed. George Steinmetz. Ithaca: Cornell University Press.

Osborne, Martin J., and Ariel Rubinstein. 1994. *A Course in Game Theory*. Cambridge: MIT Press.

Persson, Torsten, and Guido Tabellini. 2005. *The Economic Effects of Constitutions (Munich Lectures)*. Cambridge: MIT Press.

Pierson, Paul. 2000. "Three Worlds of Welfare State Research." *Comparative Political Studies* 33 (6–7): 791–821.

Pinker, Steven. 1997. *How the Mind Works*. New York: Norton.

Polachek, Solomon. 1975. "Differences in Expected Post-School Investment as a Determinant of Market Wage Differentials." *International Economic Review* 16 (2): 451–70.

———. 1978. "Sex Differences in College Major." *Industrial and Labor Relations Review* 31 (4): 498–508.

———. 1981. "Occupational Self-Selection: A Human Capital Approach to Sex Differences in the Occupational Structure." *Review of Economics and Statistics* 63 (1): 60–69.

Pollak, Robert A. 1999. "Notes on Time Use." *Monthly Labor Review* 122 (8): 7–11.

———. 2003. "Gary Becker's Contribution to Household and Family Economics." *Review of Economics of the Household* 1:111–141.

Pontusson, Jonas, Torben Iversen, and David Soskice, eds. 1999. *Unions, Employers and Central Banks: Macroeconomic Coordination and Institutional Change in Social Market Economies*. New York: Cambridge University Press.

Posner, Richard A. 1985. "An Economic Theory of the Criminal Law." *Columbia Law Review* 85 (6): 1193.

Rehfeld, Andrew. 2006. "Towards a General Theory of Political Representation," *Journal of Politics* 68 (1): 1–21.

Rich Harris, Judith. 1998. *The Nurture Assumption: Why Children Turn Out the Way They Do*. New York: Free Press.

Roemer, John. 1998. "Why the Poor Do Not Expropriate the Rich: An Old Argument in New Garb." *Journal of Public Economics* 70 (3): 99–424.

Ross, M. 2008. "Oil, Islam, and Women." *American Political Science Review* 102 (1): 107–23.

Rosenbluth, Frances, Matthew Light, and Claudia Schrag. 2004. "The Politics of Gender Equality: Explaining Variation in Fertility Levels in Rich Countries." *Women and Politics* 26 (2): 1–25.

Sanbonmatsu, Kira. 2002. "Gender Stereotypes and Vote Choice." *American Journal of Political Science* 46:20–34.

———. 2006. *Where Women Run: Gender and Party in the American States.* Ann Arbor: University of Michigan Press.

Scharpf, F. W. 2000. "Economic Changes, Vulnerabilities, and Institutional Capabilities." In *Welfare and Work in the Open Economy,* vol. 1: *From Vulnerability to Competitiveness,* ed. F. W. Scharpf and Vivien Schmidt, 21-24. New York: Oxford University Pres.

Sears, David, and J. Citrin. 1982. *Tax Revolt: Something for Nothing in California.* Cambridge: Harvard University Press.

Shapiro, Robert, and Harpreet Mahajan. 1986. "Gender Differences in Policy Preferences: A Summary of Trends from the 1960s to the 1980s." *Public Opinion Quarterly* 50:42–61.

Smith, Eric R. A. N., and Richard L. Fox. 2001. "The Electoral Fortunes of Women Candidates for Congress." *Political Research Quarterly* 54 (1): 205–21.

Squires, Judith. 1996. "Quotas for Women: Fair Representation? (Women in Politics)." *Parliamentary Affairs* 49 (1): 71(18).

Steenbergen, Marco R., and Bradford S. Jones. 2002. "Modeling Multilevel Data Structures." *American Journal of Political Science* 46 (1): 218–37.

Stockholm International Peace Research Institute. 1995. *World Armaments and Disarmament: SIPRI Yearbook.* Stockholm: SIPRI.

Studlar, Donley, Ian McAllister, and Bernadette Hayes. 1998. "Explaining the Gender Gap in Voting: A Cross-National Analysis." *Social Science Quarterly* 79 (4): 779–98.

Tedin, K. L. 1994. "Self-interest, Symbolic Values, and the Financial Equalization of the Public Schools." *Journal of Politics* 56, 628–49.

Trivers, R. L. 1971. "The Evolution of Reciprocal Altruism." *Quarterly Review of Biology* 46:35–57.

Uhlaner, Carole Jean, and Kay Lehman Schlozman. 1986. "Candidate Gender and Congressional Campaign Receipts." *Journal of Politics* 48 (1): 30–50.

UNESCO. 1999. *Operational Manual for ISCED, 1997* (International standard classification of education), 1st ed. Paris: United Nations Educational, Scientific and Cultural Organization.

Welch, Susan, and John Hibbing. 1992. "Financial Conditions, Gender, and Voting in American National Elections." *Journal of Politics* 54:197–213.

Welsh, Elaine, and Abigail Halcli. 2003. "Accounts of Feminism among Women Local Councillors in England." *Women's Studies International Forum* 26 (4): 345–56.

Zihlman, Adrienne. 1989. *The Human Evolution Coloring Book.* New York: HarperResource Press.

INDEX